T0318238

Pemba

Pemba: Spontaneous Living Spaces looks at self-built dwellings and settlements in the case study city of Pemba in the Cabo Delgado region of Mozambique.

Self-built houses born from need, in haste and with limited economical resources are often considered to be temporary structures but frequently become an integral part of the urban fabric, representative of a local culture of living. The study is part of the *Spontaneous Living Spaces* research project, and through a variety of documentation tools, it investigates the evolution of the architectural and urban elements that characterize self-built dwellings in Pemba.

The evolution of the spontaneous living culture creates new forms of living in the city connected to local cultural expressions and the environment. These are placed in relation to the traditional and contemporary living cultures, settlement trends and the natural environment.

Covering a history of housing in Mozambique and unpacking four settlement types in Pemba, this book is written for academics, professionals and researchers in architecture and planning with a particular interest in African architecture and urbanism.

Corinna Del Bianco, PhD, is an adjunct professor of urban design at the Politecnico di Milano, Italy. Her research and professional interests regard the documentation and analysis of the places' cultural identity with a focus on the culture of living in self-built urban environments. She is a founder and board member of the Fondazione Romualdo Del Bianco, a private foundation based in Florence, Italy, dedicated to dialogue among cultures.

Built Environment City Studies

The *Built Environment City Studies* series provides researchers and academics with a detailed look at individual cities through a specific lens. These concise books delve into a case study of an international city, focusing on a key built environment topic. Written by scholars from around the world, the collection provides a library of thorough studies into trends, developments and approaches that affect our cities.

Istanbul
Informal Settlements and Generative Urbanism
Noah Billig

Rio de Janeiro
Urban Expansion and Environment
José L. S. Gámez, Zhongjie Lin and Jeffrey S Nesbit

Kuala Lumpur
Community, Infrastructure and Urban Inclusivity
Marek Kozłowski, Asma Mehan and Krzysztof Nawratek

Glasgow
High-Rise Homes, Estates and Communities in the Post-War Period
Lynn Abrams, Ade Kearns, Barry Hazley and Valerie Wright

Pemba
Spontaneous Living Spaces
Corinna Del Bianco

For more information about this series, please visit: www.routledge.com/ Built-Environment-City-Studies/book-series/BECS

Pemba

Spontaneous Living Spaces

Corinna Del Bianco

Routledge
Taylor & Francis Group

LONDON AND NEW YORK

First published 2021
by Routledge
2 Park Square, Milton Park, Abingdon, Oxon OX14 4RN

and by Routledge
52 Vanderbilt Avenue, New York, NY 10017

Routledge is an imprint of the Taylor & Francis Group, an informa business

British Library Cataloguing-in-Publication Data
A catalogue record for this book is available from the British Library

Library of Congress Cataloging-in-Publication Data
Names: Del Bianco, Corinna, author.
Title: Pemba : spontaneous living spaces / Corinna Del Bianco.
Other titles: Built environment city studies.
Description: Abingdon, Oxon ; New York, NY : Routledge, 2021. |
    Series: Built environment city studies | Includes bibliographical
    references and index.
Identifiers: LCCN 2020027909 (print) | LCCN 2020027910 (ebook) |
    ISBN 9780367499976 (hardback) | ISBN 9781003048466 (ebook)
Subjects: LCSH: Architecture, Domestic—Mozambique—Pemba. |
    Housing—Mozambique—Pemba. | Pemba (Mozambique)—
    Social conditions.
Classification: LCC NA7466.6.M63 P463 2021 (print) |
    LCC NA7466.6.M63 (ebook) | DDC 728.0103096798—dc23
LC record available at https://lccn.loc.gov/2020027909
LC ebook record available at https://lccn.loc.gov/2020027910

ISBN: 978-0-367-49997-6 (hbk)
ISBN: 978-0-367-63752-1 (pbk)
ISBN: 978-1-003-04846-6 (ebk)

Typeset in Times New Roman
by Apex CoVantage, LLC

Dedicated to the people and kids of the Paquitequete, Natite, Alto Gingone and Chuiba neighbourhoods who opened their doors and welcomed me into their homes.

Contents

Figures and tables

Figures

Tables

Foreword

Michael Turner

Spontaneity has developed from its basis of philosophical thought with the writings of Kant[1] to its application in psychoanalysis and its appreciation as a culture of spontaneity especially in the fields of arts, theatre and music.

It reached out to architecture and planning with the seminal book *Architecture without Architects – an introduction to non-pedigreed architecture* by Bernard Rudofsky, accompanying the 1964 MOMA exhibition. He characterised this architecture that "(f)or want of a generic label we shall call it vernacular, anonymous, spontaneous, indigenous, rural, as the case may be".[2] However, the exhibition with 200 enlarged black and white photographs was essentially a visual exercise shown without texts or explanations. In 1969, Amos Rapoport took the next steps with his book on *House, Form and Culture* which was meant to be an exploratory study of the ways in which people organise and use dwelling space (page vii). Rapoport proposed a conceptual framework considering the spontaneity as vernacular environments using case studies from around the world. He notes that the most successful way of describing the vernacular is in terms of process – how it is "designed" and "built". Overlapping many disciplines, Rapoport already saw in the vernacular a cultural landscape and on which he subsequently published in 1992.[3]

Since then there has been much debate on the definitions of vernacular architecture while this is essentially architecture characterised by the use of local materials and knowledge, usually without the supervision of professional architects.[4] The vernacular is surely the merging of architecture and anthropology, climate, culture and materials.

The study of Spontaneous Living Spaces by Corinna Del Bianco is a journey into urban organisms with their "localization, climate, history, administrative division, population, urbanization and houses, prevailing economy, infrastructures and social systems". It is a component part of a wider global survey between the Tropic of Cancer and the Tropic of Capricorn embracing, so far, Hong Kong, Pemba and Sao Paolo. She focusses on the physical elements at the urban, architectural and technical scales and their inter-relationships, multi-sensory complexities and cultural richness. This goes beyond the urban morphological methodologies of the British school, with Conzen's work in Alnwick and of the Italian school, with Muratori's studies on Venice by adding the anthropomorphic dimension and the processes that are inherent in the evolution of the living spaces.

Corinna introduces us to Felwine Sarr in his book on Afrotopia where he follows in the footsteps of Rapoport in theorising the intangible of the cultural unseen. In an interview he said that his book project is about working on a theoretical level. Afrotopia wants to open new ways of thinking of the social, the economic, and the political realms, and of humanity itself. If you look at our African societies you can see that they are producing a lot of social innovations in many different fields. But most of these innovations happen where they are not seen, where they are not named, not thought theoretically and therefore are not noticed. "We have to challenge a mechanistic perspective and allow us to introduce new principles that of the spiritual and sensual tradition, all the symbolic capital".[5]

But the choice of Pemba is the revelation. If small and intermediate settlements are seen as "urban" with fewer than half a million inhabitants, then around 196 million people will be living in these urban centres, and in Sub-Saharan Africa – equivalent to around half of the urban population and a fifth of the total population.[6] These intermediary cities are important to Africa's future because they help connect large cities and rural areas.[7] With the projected growth of these intermediary cities in Africa it is vital to understand the potential of the fringe-belts, the repletion and replacement of the old town, and new interventions responding to evolving lifestyles.

Pemba is an intermediate coastal city and it was specifically chosen as a case study for its context in which the urbanization phenomenon is relevant but still controllable; an urban planning strategy that integrates the top-down planning with the bottom-up urban fabric that is self-constructed; and the multiple epochs of the city fabric. The engagement of the coastal towns in trade around the Indian Ocean created a syncretic culture which has left its impression on the building and living patterns, and are carefully studied in the following chapters. The Pemba case study adapts and transforms urban morphology theories of plan analysis that were developed by Michael Conzen[8] on evolutionary lines in the disciplines of geography by relating to the physical features defining the three distinct complexes of plan elements – the streets, the plots and the buildings.

Spontaneity needs to be understood in its human and physical context. In the Theatre of Spontaneity, the spontaneity player needs the spontaneous state and that of the spontaneous production.[9] Similarly, the production of living space needs the urban state that can allow the spontaneity of the community in developing these local forms.

The photographic component by Corinna addresses the notions of place and space as defined by Michel de Certeau, with the street being transformed to an animated space by the pedestrians as the intersection of moving bodies (de Certeau, 2011).[10] This was referenced by Marc Augé in his book on Non-lieux/Non-places.[11]

Rapoport develops the nature and role of Environment-Behavior Studies (EBS) in his work on Culture, Architecture and Design.[12] Here he emphasises that design must also be based on knowledge of how people and environments interact. Africa is suffering from climate extremes and Corinna warns us that this is now an urgent issue challenging this interaction. The two primary themes in Africa, rapid urbanization and the global ecological crisis, weaken urban resilience and undermine efforts to meet the UN Sustainable Development Goals and adopt the New Urban Agenda being acutely affected by climate extremes and biodiversity loss. Local knowledge and wisdoms identified in the case study may be a step in the right direction.

The conclusions highlight the relevance of the case study to address the UN Sustainable Development Goals, the UN Habitat New Urban Agenda and the UNESCO Recommendation on the Historic Urban Landscape. The UN Statistics cautions that more than half of global population growth between now and 2050 is expected to occur in Africa with the doubling of the population of Sub-Saharan Africa.

The world has to face new dynamics of urbanization. Outcomes are expected to be wide-ranging and long-term, from enriching our understanding of Africa's contribution to the wider discourse on spontaneous living spaces to increasing the potential of African intermediary cities. Their crucial role in the development of a more balanced and sustainable urban system means that intermediary cities need to become more prominent in the New Urban Agenda and its implementation.[13]

Corinna notes that her research investigates the relationship of living culture between public and private spaces in different socio-economic-cultural environments. The self-built houses born from need, from haste and from limited economical resources, with formal or informal methods, and are often thought of as temporary at the time they were built, since decades have been constituent parts of the urban fabric. Losing the character of temporariness, it becomes natural and necessary to consider them as an integral part of the city.[14] This approach is the essence of the revitalisation of African urban culture.

Rapoport summarises that there are four attitudes possible to vernacular design:[15]

1 they can be ignored
2 acknowledged but relevance denied
3 they can be copied
4 one can learn by analysing them

In support of the last attitude, he states that "spontaneous settlements are an essential part of the built environment, of the body of evidence on the basis which generalisations are made. No theory of the built environment that ignores spontaneous settlements, as most so-called architectural, urban design and landscape 'theory' does, is worthy of the name".

This book addresses the challenges of the Rapoport's fourth attitude together with the developing of theories for the unnamed social innovations of Sarr, thereby contributing to the body of circulatory knowledge on spontaneous living spaces. The transfer of knowledge will show this study to have great relevance to geo-cultural contexts beyond the East African coast.

Michael Turner,
Professor
UNESCO Chair in Urban Design and
Conservation Studies
Bezalel Academy of Arts and Design, Jerusalem

Notes

1 Kant on Freedom and Spontaneity, ed. Kate A. Moran, Cambridge University Press, 2018.
2 Rudofsky, Architecture Without Architects, page 58.
3 Rapoport, Amos. (1992). On Cultural Landscapes. *Traditional Dwellings and Settlements Review*, Volume 3, No. 2, pp. 33–47. Accessed May 27, 2020. www.jstor.org/stable/41757142.
4 Brunskill, R. W. (2000) [1971]. *Illustrated Handbook of Vernacular Architecture* (4th ed.). London: Faber and Faber.
5 Issue No 9 – Membrane; *Afrotopia or The Future is Open* with Felwine Sarr by Deniz Utlu, 30 April 2019.
6 Derived from statistics in the United Nations, World Urbanization Prospects: The 2014 Revision, POP/DB/WUP/Rev.2014/1/F09, Population Division, Department of Economic and Social Affairs, New York, 2014.
7 Maggie Chazal, founder of the NGO Urbanists Without Borders.
8 Alnwick, Northumberland: A Study in Town-Plan Analysis; M. R. G. Conzen; Transactions and Papers (Institute of British Geographers) No. 27 (1960), pp. iii+ix-xi+1+3–122 (140 pages) Published by: Wiley on behalf of The Royal Geographical Society (with the Institute of British Geographers).

9 The Theatre of Spontaneity, Jacob L. Moreno, 2010 The North-West Psycho-drama Association, UK.
10 de Certeau, M. (2011). *The Practice of Everyday Life* (3rd ed.). (S. Rendall, Trans.) Oakland, CA: University of California Press.
11 Marc Augé, Non-Places: An Introduction to Anthropology of Supermodernity, Le Seuil, 1992, Verso, p. 122.
12 Culture, Architecture, and Design, 2005, Amos Rapoport, Locke Science Publishing Co., Inc.
13 United Cities and Local Government www.uclg.org/en/agenda/intermediary-cities.
14 Spontaneouslivingspaces.com.
15 Spontaneous Shelter: International Perspectives and Prospects. Carl V. Patton Temple University Press, 1988 – pp 380 Chapter 3 Spontaneous Settlements as vernacular Design pp 51–77 Amos Rapoport.

Acknowledgements

The study stretched over several years, and many are the people who were involved and made possible its realization; to mention all of them is not possible in this framework.

Firstly, I would like to express my gratitude to my Routledge editors for guiding me in the creation of this book and to the reviewers, even though I do not know their names, for their constructive critiques and suggestions that deeply helped me in improving my manuscript.

As the Pemba case study was developed within the framework of my PhD at the Politecnico di Milano, I would like to express my gratitude to my supervisor Michele Ugolini, to the doctoral board of the DASTU Department and to the scientific community of the Politecnico di Milano, in particular to Laura Montedoro for her insightful comments and encouragement during the research, to Nora Lombardini who insisted on this publication by offering her sincere support and to Stefano Moroni who was always ready to help me find appropriate writing solutions for this book. Special thanks to Stefano Boeri, with whom I started developing the *Spontaneous Living Spaces* research project and who, since its origins, has always found words of encouragement and support.

Enormous is the gratitude to Michael Turner of the Bezalel Academy in Jerusalem; he supported my research before and during my PhD, becoming my co-supervisor. His expertise, vast knowledge and constant and patient assistance added considerably to my experience. His foreword to this book is a cause of great honour.

The research would not have been possible without the on-site survey in Mozambique, and many are the people and organizations that helped me when I was there. Therefore, a great thanks goes to UN Habitat Mozambique, USAID, the Municipality of Pemba, the ArPac de Pemba, the University UNILURIO, the Oikos NGO, the Architetti senza Frontiere team and the Associaçao de Guia de Tuchambane, in particular João Aikelevila, who was my guide during the inspections and considerably helped in the communication with dwellers.

My sincere gratitude to all the people who contributed to this work with their experience on heritage, housing, urban design and African studies: my father Paolo Del Bianco, Sandro Bruschi, Giancarlo Cataldi, Paul Jenkins, Luis Lage, Emma Mandelli, Maria Chiara Pastore, Filippo Romano and José Danilo Silvestre.

A deep and sincere thanks to my parents and my sisters who have always helped me to read my work with a different perspective.

A very special thanks to Andrea for supporting my creative energy and to my friends, Sara, Serena, Livia and Stefano, who were ready to read the drafts of this book and give me their inspiring points of view to ameliorate.

The greatest thanks go to the communities of the Paquitequete, Natite, Alto Gingone and Chuiba neighbourhoods and to all their people and kids who opened their doors and welcomed me into their homes. It is to them that this work is dedicated.

Acronyms

AIDS	Acquired Immune Deficiency Syndrome
CMCP	Conselho Municipal da Cidade de Pemba
DUAT	Direito de Uso e Aproveitamento da Terra
FRELIMO	Frente de Libertação de Moçambique
HIV	Human Immunodeficiency Virus
INE	Instituto Nacional de Estatística
INPF	Instituto National de Planeamento Fisico
MICOA	Ministry for the Coordination of Environmental Affairs
PEDM	Plano de Desenvolvimento Municipal
PEUM	Plano de Estruttura Urbana Municipal
QNP	Quirimbas National Park
RENAMO	Resistência Nacional Moçambicana
TDM	Telecommunicações de Moçambique
UNOMOZ	United Nations Operations in Mozambique
UNWTO	United Nations World Tourism Organization
USAID	United States Agency for International Development

Essential glossary

Bathroom
Constructed for the purpose of performing the activity of washing oneself. It is closer to the idea of the shower cabin in Western conception.

Capulana
Also present in some other African states, it consists of a stole measuring about 1m x 2m and is used as a skirt, baby/child carrier, bag, cloth to cover and shelter oneself, a curtain, tablecloth and has many other uses.

Chapa
Local name for metal sheets, usually constructed from zinc, used mainly for roofing.

Dhow
Traditional sailing vessel of Arab and Indian origins. Usually in Pemba it is self-built by digging out a one-piece tree trunk, and it is then used with one mast with a triangular sail.

House
Sequence of open and closed spaces within a plot in which everyday living functions are performed both in covered and uncovered spaces. Usually in the Mozambican yard a number of different constructions are present.

Latrine
Hole dug in the ground at which persons can perform physiological functions (urination and defecation).

Living room
Outdoor space where everyday activities are performed.

Macua

African ethnic group, the largest in North Mozambique and in the southern border provinces of Tanzania.

Makonde or Maconde

African ethnic group that is present in southeast Tanzania and northern Mozambique.

Matope

Vertical finishing of the *pau à pique* walls made of coloured earth.

Mwanì

Ethnic group of Arab origin that is present along the African coasts of the Indian Ocean.

Pau à pique

Vertical traditional construction technique. In Pemba it is the most diffused for self-built structures. It is made of two rows of bamboo filled with mud and pebbles.

Preface

The African continent is an effervescent field of study for the analysis of the self-built housing phenomena that represent the culture of making the home and city. Their critical study and representation allow us to imagine new urban development models reflecting the local cultural identity. The continent, so different from the rest of the globalized world for historical, cultural and economic reasons, is now experiencing an important urbanization process, and in many cases, this happens spontaneously by importing rural housing models into the city through the constructive competences of the inhabitants, thus giving life to new forms of development.

Among the African countries, Mozambique is particularly interesting for its characteristic rurality. In this context, it is possible to observe ways of living that merge rural and urban characteristics. Self-construction, which is often encouraged by the municipalities, generates ways of making cities that also create spaces for diffused production in the homes, for example, with subsistence agriculture or poultry farming. In this transition from rural to urban, however, much of the widespread traditional knowledge and many of the cultural expressions of the peasant world, full of awareness related to the environment and nature, are likely to be lost, as has widely happened in industrialized countries.

Pemba is an intermediate Mozambican city located on the coast in the far north of the country and is the capital of the Cabo Delgado region. It was established as a Swahili port settlement precisely because of its location on the Pemba Bay, which makes it a perfectly natural port that later was used also by the Europeans during the centuries of Portuguese colonization. The city is characterized by exceptional natural resources, such as kilometres of white beaches with lively coral reefs, and it is the gateway for the Quirimbas Archipelago, a natural park that since 2018 has been registered as a "biosphere reserve" on the UNESCO World Heritage List.

Pemba is limited in size, but it is experiencing a strong population increase. Precisely for these two reasons, combined with the historicity of its development, it represents an ideal case study both to observe the evolution of the Mozambican culture of living and to imagine alternative development dynamics that place the relationship between man and the environment at the centre.

The Pemba case study is part of the *Spontaneous Living Spaces* research project, which, since 2011, has been studying the ways of inhabiting self-built houses, which are intended as mirrors of the local cultural identity. *Spontaneous Living Spaces* considers spontaneous living as a fundamental element of the urban landscape and of the heritage of a place, both in its tangible and intangible forms. Therefore, its documentation and understanding, in order to preserve, communicate and enhance the diversity of the cultural expressions, is of fundamental importance.

The research is in constant evolution with new case studies in different cultural contexts for the protection of the culture of living on a global level. Cases are analyzed through field surveys and produce a variety of representation and documentation outputs, from the architectural drawings to the urban analysis and from the interviews to the photo reportage. The study on Pemba, the subject of this book, is accompanied by two case studies: one investigating the culture of living in the South American context, with research on a *favela* in Sao Paulo, and one on the Asian continent, with a study on a traditional low-density neighbourhood in Hong Kong. To date, the two represent the terms of comparison of the *spontaneous* culture of living.

1 Introduction

Spontaneous Living Spaces, a research project

Spontaneous Living Spaces[2] is a research project that was born in 2011 to investigate the culture of living through self-built houses, analyzing the relationship between public and private and environment and built up in different socio-economic and cultural contexts.

Self-building, in its formal and informal forms, represents a large part of the urban landscape in developing countries. Self-built houses arise from the need for shelter, the haste to achieve it and limited economic possibilities and are often considered temporary at the time of their construction, but then, in many cases, instead of being destroyed or abandoned, they evolve, becoming a constituent part of the city and often characterizing its landscape. Losing their initial temporary nature, it is necessary to consider these settlements as an integral part of the urban fabric; therefore, they must be recognized, documented and studied as a development stage of the urban organism in which it is possible to identify elements and characteristics of contemporary living. Furthermore, having not been designed by professionals, they represent the direct response to the local cultural needs of living, and studying them allows a greater understanding and a deeper analysis of the place of socio-cultural dynamics (Del Bianco, 2017).

The spaces' documentation and study is done through an integrated typo-morphological analysis at various scales, from the urban to the objects scales, and uses several instruments, among which is the architectural survey for spaces and functions, photo reportage, videos, interviews and historical documentation to trace the evolution of the settlements and of the houses' typologies.

To date, three case studies have been developed, and they can be compared to highlight the living spaces in different cultural contexts. The three case studies are: (1) the *favela* Guapira II in Sao Paulo, called Jardim Filhos da Terra (2), Pok Fu Lam, a historical neighbourhood of Hong Kong and (3) four selected neighbourhoods of Pemba, an intermediate Mozambican city and the object of this book.[3]

These cases represent examples of self-building in a comparable climatic zone, all of which are located between the Tropic of Cancer and the Tropic of Capricorn (Figure 1.1a). To date, the research used the climatic element to facilitate the cultural comparison but, objectifying the creation of an atlas of the spontaneous living, in the future, case studies not belonging to this area will not be excluded.[4]

Conceiving the house as a cultural phenomenon resulting from a whole range of socio-cultural factors seen in their broadest terms and adapted to local climatic conditions, site, economical possibilities, technologies and materials (Rapoport, 1969), the research considers the forms of living as cultural expressions; therefore, understanding their diversity makes it possible to gain a deeper knowledge of the context, taking into account its tangible and intangible nature and its traditional knowledge for their conservation, communication and enhancement in respect of the local cultural identity and to design, responding to culture peculiarities and to environmental interactions.

From a methodological point of view, each case study follows a specific path but always goes through three phases: (1) the preliminary documentation, (2) the field survey and (3) the consequent reorganization and analysis of the information acquired. This leads to the determination of the prevailing typologies of the surveyed area and, where possible, to detect the characteristics of variance and permanence from the traditional house. The activities of an on-site survey and contact with the local community are of fundamental importance as it is the interviewed inhabitant who, sharing her/his spaces, experience and memory, consents to the comprehension of the space, of its evolution and of its potentialities, in respect to her/his real needs. Considering that this type of documentation is particularly invasive, the action can be difficult and risky, and the modalities of involvement of the community need to be specifically tailored and then studied and tested. All of the on-site procedures were developed with the help of a local and attentive guide able to accompany and to act as a 'cultural interpreter' and, in some cases, also a linguistic one. Firstly, the guide's role is necessary to explain and let the inhabitants appreciate the research work that is aimed at the enhancement of the local culture, thus facilitating the delicate process of interpersonal knowledge that allows access to the houses which will then be documented and analyzed. For example, in the Sao Paulo case study, the main difficulty was to obtain the inhabitants' trust to engage in dialogue and to gain access to their private spaces. Therefore, the main factor in establishing this trust relationship was achieved by taking part in the local school activities and clearly explaining the study to the teachers and the kids the work to be done. In this way, they became part of the research explaining it to the other community members, allowing the establishment of the trust relationship that made the survey possible. The Chinese case study was a completely different situation as residents of Pok Fu Lam, which stands out among the districts of Hong Kong for its low density and historicity, have a strong awareness of its cultural value, so the inhabitants did not offer any resistance to the survey operations. However, the guide of the Red Cross added considerably to the on-site work, as the organization is particularly present and active within the neighbourhood. Instead, in the Mozambican case study, the difficulties were both linguistic and cultural. Therefore, it was essential to have a guide who could interpret by speaking the dialects of Makua, Makonde and Mwanì, as well as Swahili and Portuguese, fluently. In fact, frequently, the people interviewed speak dialects or minor languages on the one hand, and on the other they have unusual religious rites and beliefs that must be understood as they reflect on some of the spaces in the house.

This work of connecting with the local community reflects on the icono-graphic apparatus and on the photo reportages with portraits of the inhabit-ants taken within their houses. The photo reportage is a precious tool to represent and contextualize the research. In fact, each case study has its own photographic apparatus that can broaden the view on the inhabitants' daily lives.[5] As for the case of Mozambique, the research is accompanied by two photographic projects: *Tides* and *Capulanas*. The first gives a representation of the importance of the sea, with its tides, in the locals' daily life and family economy, while the second documents an element of the local costume, the *capulana*,[6] intended as part of the local cultural heritage.[7]

In conclusion, the documentation of the local culture of living, carried out by this research, is important for the conservation and valorization of the local knowledge, in particular as that knowledge concerns the relation-ships between the community and the surrounding natural environment, which make it considerably part of the local cultural heritage.[8] Therefore, *Spontaneous Living Spaces'* work is addressed to the inhabitants for the awareness of their cultural value, to planners and designers to design with respect for the local urban and architectural identity and for the preserva-tion of the diversity of cultural expressions, and to municipalities, GOs and NGOs working on site for a sustainable development aimed at meet-ing the objectives set by Agenda 2030. The information collected is also important for documentation purposes aimed at the recognition, conserva-tion and enhancement of forms of heritage, both tangible and intangible, which characterize the local culture and urban landscape, acknowledging the contribution of UNESCO (2003) *Convention for the Safeguarding of the Intangible Cultural Heritage* and to UNESCO (2005) *Convention on the Protection and Promotion of the Diversity of Cultural Expressions*. Finally, the results of the research are also addressed to the academic public and to research centres that investigate the topics of living, self-construction and urban design, as well as those who carry out studies on the larger scale of the Global South and developing countries.

Figure 1.1 Framing of the research case studies and localization. (a) Spontaneous living spaces location map. (b) Mozambique with highlighted Pemba and Cabo Delgado region

Source: Corinna Del Bianco

Understanding Africa's great cultural opportunity

When it comes to Africa, it is necessary first of all to keep in mind that we are talking about a continent of about 30,000,000 km^2 which represents a quarter of the emerged lands of our country, which includes 54 countries and about 1 billion people, with a growth rate of 2.6%, and, therefore, in 50 years it is expected to reach 2.2 billion, or a quarter of the world population of which, to date, only 45% lives in urban areas. In addition, the continent is made up of 60% of unused arable land and has a third of the global natural resources (Sarr, 2018).

Thinking about the development of this continent, so vast, populous and rich in resources, and to understand the reasons that led to its backwardness, it is necessary to take into account some fundamental facts that have characterized its history. For example, the continent has always been subject to 'non-determination', as the beginning of its colonization dates back to 146 B.C., when the Romans began occupying the northernmost areas. When the most recent European colonizations began in the 16th century, Africans had an important demographic advantage, as they represented, with their estimated 100 million inhabitants, 20% of the world population. This advantage was dramatically interrupted by the slave trade, which led the African population to represent, in the 19th century, just 9% of the world population (Sarr, 2018). The slave trade was one of the largest and most enduring extermination works ever carried out: it is estimated that 24 million people were relocated, and about 200 million died in the traffic due to the capture, transportation, raids and wars or diseases that were introduced by the Europeans and that exterminated entire ethnic groups with diseases such as syphilis, tuberculosis and pneumonia (Sarr, 2018).

In addition, the imposition of political and economic power on dominated cultures has further stopped the local development, which has generated 'dominated' psychological dynamics.

The colonization process in Africa did not end with independences but continued with other comparable relationships, despite the fact that once free, states acquired a greater capacity for self-determination and negotiating power. In fact, as reported by Pádraig Carmody in *The New Scramble for Africa* (Carmody, 2016), both the economic policy of colonialism and the current footprint of contemporary foreign trade, in particular the Asian one,[9] is based on natural resources,[10] and usually the benefit for the local population is little.

These are only hints to the complex factors and dynamics that have determined the disadvantage of the continent compared to the colonizing countries that now try, in various ways, to provide aid for the development of African states that is measured by their economic and social development indexes.

But in order to generate sustainable and lasting processes, development must be rooted in the local cultural matrix to be able to set context-tailored goals drawn on specific experience and history.

The Senegalese sociologist Sarr defines culture as:

> a set of practices and values, of material and spiritual traits that identify a particular social group [. . .] The cultural matrix of individuals, made up of social conventions, religious beliefs (food interdictions, clothing codes), a culinary culture, aesthetic concepts, ethical prescriptions has the function of modeling the desires (needs) of individuals and the circumstances (temporality, place) to their satisfaction.
>
> (Sarr, 2018)

In the African context, as in other colonized cultures, the dependence that favours difficulty in development is firstly cultural. For example, in most cases, the institutions are those set by the Europeans because, once independence was declared, the new African states found themselves having to manage an ethnic, economic, linguistic, religious and cultural multiplicity without having their own history and management experience of a country. Therefore, for speed and logic, trying to quickly lay the foundations for creating a national identity, it was decided to keep the institutions already present that were created by the colonial powers, as well as the language. Mozambique, for example, in 1975,[11] had to reorganize as it was facing strong ethnic diversity and a multiplicity of languages spoken[12] within the country. Therefore, at the time of its independence, it decided to elect Portuguese as its national language, which was not, and in much of the country still is not, spoken fluently by the population. However, it was the language of the already-existing institutions; it allowed access to organizations for the promotion of foreign relations, such as the Community of Lusophone countries,[13] and the maintenance of more fluid relations with the colonizing country. Another element of reflection, to understand the roots of cultural dependence, concerns the higher education systems. In general, these mirror the European systems and programmes without being truly linked to local culture.

Following these reflections, which can be extended to many other spheres, the risk is that on the one hand local culture risks being lost, and on the other the development system, not being rooted in the local cultural matrix, will not lead to a lasting and sustainable development process. "Economy and development are cultural processes. The development of African economies needs to be anchored to their cultural context", says Sarr in *Afrotopia* (Sarr, 2018).

Therefore, it is necessary to enhance local cultural forms, documenting them, improving and conveying them and protecting them from globalization because it is on these that the identity and therefore the wealth of a people are formed for its development. For example, literature, music, fashion and visual arts, such as painting, photography and cinema, as well as architecture and urban design, are fundamental in composing the mosaic of expressions of a cultural context. Africa abounds in these, but a part, the one considered 'poor' or 'rural', is not sufficiently valued, and the other part often develops from and for a Western public, recalling an 'exotic taste' and not for its free cultural development.

Even on an urban scale, meaning the city as a living organism, made up of a set of social, economic and architectural elements that represent the culture of those who inhabit it, African cities must represent the identity of the people who live in them, with their history and aspirations. This is not always reflected in urban and architectural projects that aspire to forms, materials, functions and lifestyles of international inspiration. On the contrary, each part of the city needs to be related to its spontaneous and vernacular matrix which can be conceived as a direct translation into the physical form of a culture, its needs, values, desires, dreams and the passions of its people (Rapoport, 1969).

For these reasons, the analysis and documentation of traditional forms of living are crucial, both in their urban and rural dimensions, as well as their 'spontaneous' transformation and their adaptation to the urbanization dynamics. The widespread self-construction represents a relevant contemporary way of living and has to be recorded at various scales, from the living cell to the urban one. Generally speaking, in self-construction the use of traditional forms and spaces is frequent, handed down orally from generation to generation, as well as local and vegetal materials which today, in the urban context, are starting to be replaced with industrial ones. The close relation between the architectural forms and the local culture makes the typologies uniform and long-lasting (Rapoport, 1969), and this is clearly visible in the detected prevailing typologies. Spontaneous answers to the need for a home, and their aggregation, can give important ideas and information to designers who aim for sustainable and integrated planning with local culture, which does not impose a lifestyle but aims at improving the existing one, using the ability of the inhabitants to take part in self-construction.

Finally, it is necessary for architects as well as, more broadly, all African professionals, to recognize their cultural value. They are the actors who can re-think a development rooted in their own identity and not led by foreigners because, as attentive as they are to context, they will never be able to create a process of cultural development comparable to the one that local professionals can generate with their excellent work.

A glance at Mozambique

In the framework of Sub-Saharan Africa, Mozambique is a territory that has always been part of the world linked to trade along the Indian Ocean, with Indian, Arab and Gulf merchants, and then the Europeans, on the one hand, with the Portuguese occupation on the coasts, and on the other with the British missions in the interior.

Located on the eastern coast of the African continent, separated from the Madagascar island by the Mozambique Channel, the Republic of Mozambique is bordered by Tanzania to the north, Malawi and Zambia to the northwest, Zimbabwe to the west, Swaziland and South Africa to the southwest, and the Indian Ocean, with a coastline of over 2,800 km. The country was a former Portuguese colony and gained independence in 1975, with the guerrilla forces of the Frente de Libertação de Moçambique (FRELIMO) who, from independence to today, lead the country. Until 1898 the capital of the Portuguese colony was the Island of Mozambique in the Nampula region and which, since 1991, has been declared a UNESCO World Heritage Site.[14] The island is approximately 140 maritime miles from Pemba and about 400 km by land route. Today the capital of the country is Maputo, previously named Lorenço Marquez, which is located on the southern coast.

After independence, from 1977 until 1992, the country faced a violent civil war that destroyed the country from the social, economic and cultural points of view. The main actors of this fight were the FRELIMO, which tried to establish a socialist one-state party, and the Mozambican National Resistance (RENAMO), the anti-communist party supported by Rhodesia and South Africa. In those years the country, which, because of its colonial past, did not have a prosperous economy, was completely destroyed. Over 1 million people died during the conflicts or because of hunger, and the few existing infrastructures (rural streets, hospitals, rail lines, schools and so on) were destroyed.[15] The civil war ended with the Rome General Peace Accords, signed in Rome by the second Mozambican President Joaquim Chissano and the RENAMO President Afonso Dhalakama. To ensure the implementation of the Rome General Peace Accords, the UN established a mission, called United Nations Operations in Mozambique (UNOMOZ). This mission lasted from October 1992 until December 1994,[16] and, according to Berdal, the mission was successful, despite the numerous obstacles they had to face (Koops et al., 2015). Since the end of the civil war, the country has been living in a period of general peace, with the exception of new tensions that emerged between FRELIMO and RENAMO between 2013 and 2018, which ended with the peace agreements of August 1, 2019, signed by President Filipe Nyusi and RENAMO leader Ossufo Momade.

Furthermore, since 2018, in the region of Cabo Delgado, the Insurgency in Cabo Delgado, a conflict between Islamists and the Mozambican security forces is ongoing. The Islamic militants[17] fight to establish an Islamic state in the Cabo Delgado region and are attacking mainly civilians in villages, causing death and destruction, and, as West mentions, according to some reports, it brought a halt to development in the area (West, 2018).

The country has an abundance of resources, including kilometres of white beaches and coral reefs, coal, graphite and natural gas deposits, seas rich in fish and ports. Despite these riches, the 2019 Human Development Index[18] ranks it 180th out of 189 countries. Life expectancy is 60.2 years, education 3.5 years (compared to 9.7 years expected), with over half of the population living on less than $1.50 a day. To this must be added a high unemployment rate, especially for young people. But Mozambique is one of the major recipients of international aid in the world, and in recent decades this has been growing steadily (in 1981, they received $158 million; in 1987, $735 million; in 1990, $1.061 billion), and currently this represents about 41% of the gross domestic product (GDP). Finally, between 1992 and 1994, the United Nations UNOMOZ project, as well as many NGO projects, helped to widen the social gap as local staff from international projects generally receive above-average salaries (Newitt, 2017).

Furthermore, Mozambique today attracts international interests for large projects involving important foreign investments. These include, for example, the Mozal aluminium plant in Maputo, in which South Africa is involved, the construction of large infrastructures, in which Chinese involvement is fundamental, including a new railway line, the expansion of the port of Nacala, large-scale commercial cultivations and finally projects on natural resources, including coal[19] and liquid natural gas (LNG), of which large deposits have recently been discovered in the marine area of the Cabo Delgado region. The region, whose capital is Pemba, is located along the coast in the far north of the country and is rich in natural and landscape resources, such as the Quirimbas National Park (QNP). In 2010, the size of the gas reserves was determined, which places Mozambique among the top ten countries for this resource. The extraction and liquefaction investments began in 2011, mainly with two projects: the first by the US company Anadarko with onshore platforms in the Afungi Peninsula in the far north of the country about 300 km north of Pemba, and the second by the Italian company ENI with offshore extraction fields (Symons, 2016). At the end of 2019, Anadarko sold its shares to the French Total (WorldOil.com), and to date, in addition to this, the Mozambique LNG Project sees among its actors the Japanese MITSUI & Co., the Indian INGC, the Mozambican national oil company ENH, Mumbai-based Bharat PetroResources, Thai PTT Public Plc and Oil India Limited, the second largest Indian oil and gas company. The project compensates for the exploitation of natural resources with socio-economic development incentives in the area aimed at raising health, educational, environmental, community and philanthropic conditions and regional development initiatives. Finally, the project involves the relocation, with compensation policies, of the population of the Afungi Peninsula, where the LNG park will be built.[20]

As regards the projects of the Italian company ENI, these operate on the Rovuma offshore basins with the super-giant deposits Coral, Mamba and Agulha.[21] Since May 2019, the company has obtained, together with a team of other operators, the exploration and development rights of the deep waters of the Angoche and Zambezi basins, and its extraction plan has been approved. It is believed that the activities aimed at the commercialization of the LNG park will begin in 2024. Also, in this case, the project foresees the creation of programmes to compensate the local population, in particular in health care services, education and the replacement of coal stoves with electric ones.[22]

As Anderson mentions, already in 2012, it was highlighted how powerful, for the country's economic boom, the development of the hydrocarbon industry could have been, but, at the same time, also how strong the risk was of creating a new resources exploitation system, by foreign investments, which would not have left real wealth to the local population (Anderson, 2012). In fact, the projects have also given rise to a series of complaints, mainly related to the relocation of communities living in the Afungi Peninsula and to the growth of the cost of living (Symons, 2016).

Finally, Mozambique must also address large-scale environmental issues, including forests (in particular of ironwood and ebony) that are being cut, illegal hunting and fishing that are emptying reserves and seas, the Zambezi dams that are dramatically altering the ecology of the river valley, illegal gold washing that destroys the landscape, as well as the cyclic and dramatic episodes related to climate extremes, such as the two cyclones called Idai and Kenneth, which, in 2019, affected the whole country and in particular the region of Cabo Delgado. These, with their impact on population and houses, will be discussed in Chapter 4.

One wonders why the country cannot raise its economy; as Newitt describes, there are many theories: those who think that the former colonial rule is still the cause of underdevelopment, those who blame the socialist Soviet-style development policies established after independence, some on civil war and some on the global economy. There is certainly a causal overlap, but perhaps, as mentioned previously, taking into consideration a wider field, the problem can also be traced to the development approach based on Western cultural matrices instead of allowing the evolution of a new and context-related development model. It is clear that the international economic system does not make this process easy, but probably, if a country like Mozambique manages to enhance its culture through its socio-economic development, it could make a significant contribution to global cultural development. For example, this is a land still very rich in cultural expressions and traditional knowledge, which are closely linked, and with deep respect for the environment and nature. This diffused knowledge, with resilient houses that are a demonstration of self-building and self-production, represents a wealth that has been lost in urbanized countries and that even in Mozambique, which is going through an important transition from a rural to an urban country, is in danger of being lost and therefore must be protected in order to imagine an alternative development model to that of the 'city system'. This also represents an opportunity for developed countries that have experienced industrialization and who are now experiencing the crisis of the urban system with its problems of pollution, congestion, climate extremes and access to resources.

The following research work is part of this picture, a work that starts from the analysis of the self-built living cell with its materials, spaces and objects, its inhabitants and builders and their way of developing their neighbourhood and city. The research is based on a field survey in four selected neighbourhoods of Pemba, which is a Mozambican intermediate city located in a bay and a natural port on the coast of the Cabo Delgado region (Figure 1.1b). As previously mentioned, it is part of the larger *Spontaneous Living Spaces* research project of which it represents a piece in the composition of the global mosaic of the self-built forms of living.

Notes

1 www.spontaneouslivingspaces.org.
2 The project website is www.spontaneouslivingspaces.com; further information on the research and collateral projects can be found at www.corinnadelbianco.com.
3 The Sao Paulo case study was developed in 2012 under the supervision of Stefano Boeri and Pier Paolo Tamburelli and with the support of the Municipality of Sao Paulo and was published within the book *Jardim Filhos da Terra* edited by Pacini Editore in 2014 (Del Bianco, 2014 and Lejano and Del Bianco, 2018). In 2013, the Hong Kong case study was analyzed with the help of the University of Hong Kong and the local Red Cross. Finally, the Pemba case study was developed within the framework of the PhD, concluded with *laude* in December 2018, at the Politecnico di Milano, under the supervision of Michele Ugolini (Associate Professor at the Politecnico di Milano, Italy) and Michael Turner (UNESCO Chair in Urban Design and Conservation Studies, Bezalel Academy, Jerusalem, Israel).
4 Houses' forms are often more related to local culture rather than to climatic conditions (Rapoport, 1969).
5 In this book, for scientific and editorial reasons, the iconographic apparatus has been selected.

6 The *capulana*, frequently used in many African countries, is a stole of about 1m × 2m characterized by bright colours and traditional designs and is used as a skirt, baby/child carrier, bag, cloth to cover and shelter oneself, a curtain, tablecloth and has many other uses.

7 The full photo reportages are visible on the website www.corinnadelbianco.com. The photo reportage relating to the case of San Paolo was published as well in the aforementioned Pacini Editore publication and also in the scientific journal iQuaderni of Urbanistica3 number 21, published by Quodlibet, full photo essay and cover image.

8 Using two assets of categories, one for the process and one for the product, Rapoport demonstrated the similarity of spontaneous shelters to vernacular settlements rather than to highly designed ones (Rapoport, 1988, pp. 54–55).

9 The main Asian actors in Africa are China, Japan and India.

10 Since in many cases, the African coins are nonconvertible, an exchange of resources is often carried out (Carmody, 2016).

11 Mozambique gained its independence from the Portuguese colonial power in 1975.

12 Mozambique is a country of linguistic minorities; each citizen speaks at least two languages, and, among linguists, there is no agreement on the number of languages used in the territory as the boundary between dialect and language is not well defined. The number of recognized languages varies between 17 and 42, and there is a reasonable assent among linguists on 22 languages, including Portuguese. The main linguistic prevalences are Makua in the northernmost regions and Shangana in the far south (respectively spoken by 26% and 11% of the population) (Newitt, 2017).

13 The Community of Lusophone Countries (CPLP Comunidade dos Países de Lingua Portuguesa) was founded in 1996. It includes Angola, Brazil, Cape Verde, Guinea Bissau, Equatorial Guinea, Mozambique, Portugal, São Tomé, Príncipe and Timor Leste. www.cplp.org last visited March 2, 2020.

14 Mozambique joined UNESCO in October 1976. It has one cultural site inscribed in the UNESCO World Heritage List (the Island of Mozambique https://whc.unesco.org/en/list/599/) and one protected as a biosphere reserve (the Quirimbas National Park https://en.unesco.org/biosphere/africa/quirimbas). On the tentative list are other four properties, among which are two cultural, the Manyikeni and Chibuene (submitted in 1997) and the Vumba Mountain Range (submitted in 2008), one natural, the Ponta de Ouro Protected Marine Area, and one mixed, the Quirimbas National Park (both submitted in 2008) http://whc.unesco.org/en/statesparties/MZ.

15 In addition, RENAMO was accused of committing human rights violations, for example, kids were used as soldiers and there was mining in the countryside.

16 The mandate included facilitating the implementation of the Agreement; monitoring the ceasefire; monitoring the withdrawal of foreign forces and providing security in the transport corridors; providing technical assistance and monitoring the entire electoral process. https://web.archive.org/web/20040811204331/www.un.org/Depts/dpko/dpko/co_mission/onumoz.htm.

17 The groups fighting for Islamism mainly belong to the religious movement Ansar al-Sunna, active in the region since 2015, first as a religious movement and then becoming militarized. The groups' leaders have religious, military and commercial links with fundamentalists of Kenya, Somalia, Tanzania and the African Great Lakes Region (West, 2018). Their fights started being claimed by the Islamic State of Iraq and the Levant (ISIL) in June 2019.

18 http://hdr.undp.org/en/content/human-development-index-hdi last visited February 29, 2020.
19 The largest coal mine in the world is located in Mozambique and is managed by the Brazilian Companhia Vale do Rio Doce. It began production in 2011.
20 www.mzlng.com last visited March 2, 2020.
21 It is about 2400 billion m³ of gas discovered between 2011 and 2014. www.eni.com last visited March 2, 2020.
22 The use of coal as a primary source for cooking food is one of the main reasons for deforestation in Mozambique. www.eni.com last visited March 2, 2020.

Reference list

Books

Carmody, P. (2016). *The New Scramble for Africa*. Second Edition. Cambridge: Polity.
Cataldi, G. (2015). *Abitazioni Primitive – Primitive Dwellings*. Firenze: Aión Edizioni.
Del Bianco, C. (2014). *Jardim Filhos da Terra*. Pisa: Pacini Editore.
Newitt, M. (2017). *A Short History of Mozambique*. London: C. Hurst & Co. Ltd.
Pillai, J. (2013). *Cultural Mapping: A Guide to Understanding Place, Community and Continuity. Strategic Information and Research Development Centre*. Selangor: SIRD Strategic Information and Research Development Centre.
Rapoport, A. (1969). *House form and Culture*. Englewood Cliffs, NJ: Prentice-Hall.
Rapoport, A. (1988). *Spontaneous Shelter*. Philadelphia: Temple University Press.
Rapoport, A. (2005). *Culture, Architecture, and Design*. Chicago: Locke Science Publishing Co.
Sarr, F. (2018). *Afrotopia*. Bologna: Edizioni dell'asino.

Documents and reports

Anadarko, ENI. (2017). *Resettlement Implementation Process*.
ONU. (2016). *Pretoria Declaration for Habitat III "Informal Settlements"*.
ONU. (2017). *New Urban Agenda, Quito Declaration on Sustainable Cities and Human Settlements for All*.
UNESCO. (2003). *Convention for the Safeguarding of the Intangible Cultural Heritage*.
UNESCO. (2005). *Convention on the Protection and Promotion of the Diversity of Cultural Expressions*.
UNESCO. (2011). *Historic Urban Landscape Recommendation*.
UN Habitat. (2014). *The State of African Cities 2014: Re-imagining Sustainable Urban Transitions*.

Articles and briefings

Anderson, E. J. (2012). What does Hydrocarbon Wealth mean for Foreign Aid in Mozambique?. *Policy Briefing 50. Global Powers and Africa Programme*. SAIIA. www.africaportal.org/publications/what-does-hydrocarbon-wealth-mean-for-foreign-aid-in-mozambique/.

Del Bianco, C. (2017), Living in Pemba Between Public and Private Space, a Morpho – Typological Field Study of Selected Neighbourhoods. In Giuseppe Amoruso (ed.), *Putting Tradition into Practice: Heritage, Place and Design, Proceedings of 5th INTBAU International Annual Event*. Milano: Springer, pp. 1423–1431. https://doi.org/10.1007/978-3-319-57937-5.

Koops, J., Tardy, T., MacQueen, N., Williams, P., and Berdal, M. (2015). United Nations Operation in Mozambique (ONUMOZ). In *The Oxford Handbook of United Nations Peacekeeping Operations*. Oxford: Oxford University Press. www.oxfordhandbooks.com/view/10.1093/oxfordhb/9780199686049.001.0001/oxfordhb-9780199686049-e-40.

Lejano, R. P., and Del Bianco, C. (May 2018). The Logic of Informality: Pattern and Process in a São Paulo Favela. *Geoforum*, Volume 91. Elsevier, pp. 195–205. https://doi.org/10.1016/j.geoforum.2018.03.005.

Rapoport, A. (1992). On Cultural Landscapes. *Traditional Dwellings and Settlements Review*, Volume 3, No. 2, pp. 33–47.

Symons, K. (2016). Transnational Spaces, Hybrid Governance and Civil Society Contestation in Mozambique's Gas Boom. *The Extractive Industries and Society*, Volume 3, pp. 149–159.

West, S. (2018). Ansar al-Sunna: A New Militant Islamist Group Emerges in Mozambique. *Terrorism Monitor*, Volume XVI, No. 12, pp. 5–7.

Websites

Community of Lusophone Countries | www.cplp.org
Corinna Del Bianco | www.corinnadelbianco.com
ENI Spa | www.eni.com
Home Space Maputo project | www.homespace.dk
InfoAfrica | www.infoafrica.it
iQuaderni di U3 | www.urbanisticatre.uniroma3.it/dipsu/?page_id=17
Mozambique LNG | www.mzlng.com
Population Statistics for Countries, Administrative Areas, Cities and Agglomerations – Interactive Maps and Charts | www.citypopulation.de/Mocambique.html
Spontaneous Living Spaces | www.spontaneouslivingspaces.com
UN Development Programme Humand Development Reports | www.hdr.undp.org
UNESCO | www.unesco.org
WorldOil online magazine | www.worldoil.com

2   Studying Mozambican self-built houses in the city of Pemba

The relevance of the current housing issue in Mozambique

World population is increasing, and cities are growing exponentially, especially in those countries that are currently facing the industrialization process. Trends suggest that by 2100, 70% of people will live in cities (ONU, 2015). If this happens, we will have to deal with new dynamics.

At the global level, the movement to cities is fostered by two main factors: the growth of the total population and immigration from rural areas. Southern Africa is now facing this urbanization phenomenon.

With a density of 37 people every square kilometre in 2016 (Data World Bank, 2016), and with an urban population of 36%, which is growing every year with an increase from 3.2% to 5%, Mozambique represents a relevant context in which urban and architectural development issues can be studied.

According to the projections, Mozambique will reach its urban majority by 2050. Therefore, the country is interesting on one side for its contemporary rural forms of living and on the other because of its evolutionary process, which can be mapped, recorded and analyzed at this stage of development.

Mozambican cities have a wide range of foundation times and origins, and in all cases, housing is a major issue. Today, in cities, the control that the authorities have over the arriving population is limited. This is due to the elevated speed of the urbanization process, and therefore it is difficult to monitor the self-construction of houses, both formal and informal.

Usually people who arrive to the city need a shelter in a short time and have a rural background that gives them the capability to build their own houses. Municipalities often face the difficulty of providing a shelter in time and at affordable prices to all those who arrive in the city. This justifies why informality and slums characterize most of the developing cities (UN Habitat, 2007).

The informal development of the cities can be considered an outdated process of urbanization that was born with the same concept of 'city'. Self-built houses constitute the main part of the urban landscape in developing countries. Considering their relevance, they require a deeper analysis of the present typologies and a comprehension of the features of variance and permanence from the traditional living typology. In time, some features evolved (in terms of materials, shape, function and so on), creating a variance from the traditional typology, while other features may have preserved the original characteristics constituting the permanence characteristics of the typology. This process happened both at the urban and architectural scale.

Globalization is a factor that is influencing the living typology in terms of city investments, new economies (such as gas, oil and tourism) and architectural functions, elements and materials.

Therefore, the research recognizes the importance of self-built architecture within the urban fabric, analyzing the relationships between house and street and city dynamics, looking at the urban morphology and typologies. The integrated analysis is a strong tool to recognize and understand the evolution of an urban environment. The knowledge acquired from this study leads to a stronger awareness of the distance between the Western categories and the local urban phenomena and therefore to a more conscious and culturally integrated urban plan and architectural design.

Pemba and its relevance in the dwelling issue

Mozambique is facing an important demographic growth: in 1960 it counted 7,493,278 people, and in 2015, there were 27,977,863 people (World Bank, 2016).

Pemba is the capital of the northern region of Cabo Delgado, with a surface of 98,97 km^2; it represents 8% of the population of the region (INE, 2007). The city is living the urbanization phenomenon. In 1930, it counted 2,000 people; in 1960, there were 22,000; and just after independence in 1980, there were 43,000 people. Its growth was continuous until it rose to 196,492 inhabitants in 2015. With this growth rate, the municipality is expecting to reach 323,127 inhabitants by 2024 (Conselho Municipal Da Cidade De Pemba e Micoa/Dnapot, 2014).

Since this research is a methodological reflection, it is possible to extend part of the results of this study to the Mozambican intermediate cities, among which Pemba was chosen as a representative.

In its history, Pemba, previously called Porto Amelia, was always relevant because of its strategic coastal location as it is possible to observe in the satellite image in Figure 2.1 where the selected neighbourhoods' position is also indicated. Today, the reasons for Pemba's development are mainly related to two economic factors: foreigner investments in oil and gas, and tourism.

This case study was chosen for the following reasons:

1　It is a context in which the urbanization phenomenon is relevant but still controllable;
2　In the late colonial period, Pemba started an urban planning strategy that integrates top-down planning with bottom-up (self-construction), facilitating the right to the land with local legislation (DUAT);
3　The majority of the urban fabric is self-constructed;
4　The city fabric has different ages. The research chose four survey areas, selected because they represent the living space in four different periods of expansion: (1) from the first Swahili settlement (1st–5th century), (2) to the colonial period (1498–1975), (3) from the first independence (1975–1992), (4) to the contemporary expansion (1992–2016). Therefore, the research could analyze the dwellings and settlement patterns of four phases of the city evolution at the study stage (2016) with an on-site survey and analysis.

The neighbourhoods studied in Pemba are representative of the residential areas of the city, where the majority of the popular[1] class lives. In Pemba, 53 selected homes were surveyed in their functions, spaces, architectural and urban elements. Of these houses, 40 were able to be surveyed with an equal level of detail and were reported within the case study analysis. There are 6 to 18 houses located in each of the four districts of the city, chosen because they represent the four stages of the city's evolution. In addition to the private space, the public space was also surveyed. All of the surveyed houses are formal as they are regulated by the local authority but can be considered slums[2] as in the majority of the cases they lack housing durability and adequate sanitation systems, and few of them have access to safe water and electricity.

This context has remained anchored to rural models and traditional knowledge, which now become an asset that generates lifestyles that may provide inspiration for evolutionary models that are an alternative to those of traditional urbanism.

The selection of houses and blocks was done after a preliminary visual survey of the entire neighbourhood, from which it was possible to state that the chosen samples are representative of the whole neighbourhood and provide an accurate representation of the forms of living in the local community. Their significance was also confirmed by the community leaders, the municipality staff, the UN Habitat Mozambique and USAID representatives.

The analysis was integrated with interviews conducted with the houses' inhabitants, with the neighbourhoods' leaders and with data collection on the historical architectural typologies evolution and urban development and with the municipality city vision. Due to the difficulties in translating from the Macua, Makonde and Mwani languages to Swahili and then to Portuguese, the interviews were not entirely recorded but were dutifully noted by the author. For this reason they are not integrally reported in this paper.

In addition to the on-site survey, a number of bibliographical sources were consulted. Among these were the PhD thesis *Instrumento de planeamento para cidades médias moçambicanas: o caso de Pemba* by R. P. S. Pereira (University of Lisbon) and the *Plano Estrategico de Desenvolvimento 2014–2018* of the Municipality of Pemba, with the related regulation, statistics and analysis made by the municipality itself and the Instituto Nacional de Estatística .[3] Also consulted were the studies by Jorge Dias, Sandro Bruschi and Luis Lage on the history of houses and of the city and those by Julio Carrilho and Paul Jenkins for the definition of the residential typologies in Mozambique (in Lichinga and in Maputo).

Since the 20th century, the Municipality of Pemba has been controlling the urban growth with the definition and rental of pre-drawn plots in which the inhabitants self-built their houses. Therefore, at the present time, Pemba is representative of a development that is the combination of a top-down approach and the self-building process. For this reason, the informal episodes in the urban fabric have been limited and are not representative of the city's evolution process, while the houses taken into account in the analysis are part of formal neighbourhoods. The local urbanization was not drawn, documented, nor planned in the previous phases of occupation. However, it is possible to assume from historical pictures that it was present. Furthermore, in Pemba, it is possible to observe the evolution of the houses' typologies from the first Swahili settlement to the actual prevailing settlement, documenting the architectural features of variance and permanence.

Most of the available information sources state that the European concept of urban form did not exist before the Swahili occupation but was developed with the Portuguese colonization (Bruschi and Lage, 2005). The local population has always been living and working mainly in the rural areas, and this trend is still present in the country. During the Portuguese colonization, locals were living in the suburbs of the Baixa and Cimento neighbourhoods in pre-designed and regulated plots.

The Mozambican city, as we know it today, was born after independence (June 25, 1975) when, as in most of the African socialist countries, the newly born governing party FRELIMO was imposing the Villagization Policy to control and activate the population that was living scattered around the territory. Before independence there is scarce information regarding the neighbourhoods inhabited by locals, but from a few historical illustrations and a 1969 survey, conserved at the municipality department of agriculture, it is possible to see the drawings of a few areas of the city with descriptions of the plots and street dimensions.

The Villagization Policy was a tentative solution of the political power to gather people within organized settlements for the purpose of security and control. People were first invited, then forced, to build their own houses in cities, following urban schemes imposed by the authorities that were supposed to include the basic infrastructures (mainly mobility, education and health services).

As the Villagization Policy was used by other African countries after their independence, in order to create the basis of their own cities, the results of this political strategy were not homogeneous: from the great success of the Ujiama in Tanzania to the great failure of the Ethiopian tentative solution (Lorgen, 2000).

According to research conducted by Christy Cannon Lorgen of Oxfam and published in her 2000 article "The Experience of Villagisation: Lessons from Ethiopia, Mozambique, and Tanzania":

> Over time, the forced villages led to antagonism against Frelimo. One of the biggest debates in the discourse about villagisation in Mozambique is the extent to which popular resentment of the programme inspired support for Renamo (Vines, 1991; Newitt, 1995; Finnegan, 1992; Penvenne, 1998). In areas where people were particularly unhappy with villagisation, Renamo found a population "with no great desire to inform on them, even an active welcome" (Vines, 1991). In the northern province of Nampula, Renamo had its greatest successes in those areas where villagisation had been most extensive.
>
> (Finnegan, 1992, p. 277)
>
> Particularly susceptible were youths who found their own social and educational advancement blocked by the lineage elders who dominated the Frelimo power structure in the villages. Youth may also have seen Renamo as an exciting alternative to life in the villages – or at least as a source of food. Villagisation led to unexpected social stratification in Mozambique, which Renamo was able to exploit to obtain support (Vines, 1991). The debate over the contribution of Frelimo agrarian policy to Renamo successes is far from settled; the links between the two were probably more apparent in some areas than in others and may be more a sign of discontent with Frelimo than any active interest in Renamo. The important point for this study is that forced villagisation can create considerable popular dissent. It has been argued that Frelimo progressively lost touch with the rural areas (Abrahamsson and Nilsson, 1995).
>
> (Lorgen, 2000)

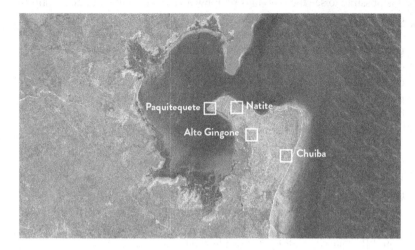

Figure 2.1 Satellite image of the Pemba Bay. Location of the surveyed
    neighbourhoods

Source: base image Google Maps

Today Pemba's city masterplan 2014–2018 and vision are not taking into
account the relationship between the prevailing houses' typology and the
possible urban evolution. However, it is necessary to recognize that the
actual masterplan is dealing with huge problems in terms of hygiene and
sanitation. Malaria and cholera are among the main causes of death. Furthermore, the issues connected to climate change are very harsh and every
year create more and more problems, especially in relation to floods and
storms (UN Habitat, USAID, CMCP, 2016).

Research goals

The research, in the framework of the New Urban Agenda – Quito Declaration on Sustainable Cities and Human Settlements for All – and of the Sustainable Development Goals, is aimed at contributing to the comprehension
of the urban issues.

In order to work in developing contexts, it is necessary to avoid the application of the Western categories and therefore the intervention methodologies.
Categories such as formal/informal, planned/unplanned and historical/con-
temporary are distorted by a context that has experienced an evolutionary process different from the Western one. For this reason, the research has drawn
attention to self-built neighbourhoods whose urban structure dates back to
different historical periods and in which the majority of the population lives.

In particular, the research will increase knowledge and therefore aware-ness of the urbanization process in Pemba. This will give the planners and designers operating in Pemba, or in Mozambican intermediate cities urban contexts, new tools to comprehend the history of the city and there-fore to design with respect for the local urban and architectural identity in order to preserve the diversity of their cultural expressions. Furthermore, the research could contribute to the NGOs working on site to implement projects with the involvement of the population in mind. In particular, the research would be useful for the improvement of living conditions and building techniques and would encourage sustainable forms of tourism and increase the awareness of the relevance of traditional construction methods and the preservation of the urban and cultural landscape.

The research observes the urban structure and living spaces of Pemba in order to analyze the process of urbanization at a controllable scale. The aim of the study is two-fold: firstly, it acknowledges that popular self-built houses are a consistent part of the urban fabric of most of the African cities and constitute the landscape of the majority of the urban contexts. There-fore, it gives self-built architecture the dignity of being studied, as any other part of the city, as bottom-up urbanization has already created the urban environments that we consider of high cultural and aesthetic value today. Secondly, it fills the gap of knowledge on the topic of houses' typologies and urban morphology in Pemba, studying the characteristics of living in the contemporary popular architecture, understanding the elements of vari-ance and permanence from the rural and traditional typology.

The research is aimed at giving a possible alternative vision for the urban development of Pemba through the implementation of the traditional self-built house typology. Therefore, it is providing an answer to a set of ques-tions that, taken together, present a view on the dwellings and settlements at the present time and in their evolution in the process of urbanization, such as:

1 What are the characteristics of living in Pemba?
2 How do the houses' typologies relate to the urban fabric and to the street? What are the existing relationships between covered and uncov-ered and public and private spaces?
3 What are the features of variance and permanence from the traditional typology to the contemporary one, and how have the city development dynamics influenced the houses' evolution over time?

Methodology and essential literature review

For the documentation and analysis of the prevailing typologies in the neighbourhoods of Pemba, the main methodological references are related to the typo-morphological schools of urban and architectural analysis, both the Italian school, with Muratori's studies on Venice, and the British school, with Conzen's work in Alnwick. Other surveys were taken into account, such as the CIAM grid and studies (especially those of Simounet in the bidonvilles of Algeri) and the inquiry *Inquérito à Arquitectura Regional Portuguesa* on popular Portuguese architectural elements by the Portuguese architects' group AAC (AAP, 1980). The architectural method was integrated with anthropological tools of analysis, photo reportages and videos. For this purpose, the bibliography was implemented with scripts of Claude Lévi-Strauss, of Marc Augé and of Janet Pillai methodological studies on cultural mapping, recognized by UNESCO (Pillai, 2013). Therefore, it was possible to represent the diversity of cultures within the city with a synoptic picture of them with the consciousness that, as Lévi-Strauss affirms, no culture is capable of giving a true judgement on another one and that it is only possible to give a representation of them (Lévì-Strauss, 2017).

Being aware of the complexity of the urban organism, the research tries to represent the current situation and evolution of the dwellings and settlements in Pemba with an analysis that integrates the study on the urban morphology and houses' typologies with six scales of details: (1) the regional framework at various scales, (2) the territorial analysis at the scale of 1:5000 – looking at the selected layers that create the city, such as the main streets, secondary streets and street fronts, (3) the neighbourhoods analysis at 1:1000 – through the layers: green, voids/built-up, infrastructures, public/private property, community functions – (4) the blocks survey analysis at the scale of 1:500, looking at the relationships between public and private and open and closed spaces and the connection elements among them, (5) the houses' spaces and functions at 1:200 and (6) the photographic survey of the elements (divided in: main structure, roof, walls, openings, hygiene, technical equipment – water and energy supply, waste collection, textures) and objects within the houses (categorized as water related, fire related, food related, living related). Exceptions found in each layer of analysis were also recorded. Furthermore, the analysis integrates the historical reconstruction of house and settlement development with historical maps. Finally, it is completed with the interaction with the local community, surveying the main cultural features characterizing the family nucleus and its relationship with the house and the neighbourhood's dynamics.

For editorial reasons, the images apparatus, describing the full survey and therefore representing the multiplicity of forms of living, was highly reduced and in this book is reported as a significant selection of the figurative work.

The literature consulted for the integrated analysis carried out in Pemba interlaces four main areas of research.

The first intersected area of research concerns the methods of survey of the buildings and the urban forms made by the English and the Italian schools of the second half of the 20th century. The 1960 work of Saverio Muratori in Venice with his *Studi per un'Operante Storia Urbana di Venezia* (Muratori, 1960) and Michael Robert Günter Conzen's 1969 studies on the urban form of Alnwick (Conzen, 2012), constitute an important base for carrying out this research, along with Gianfranco Caniggia and Gian Luigi Maffei's work on the reading of the urban fabric with an inter-scalar methodology (Caniggia and Maffei, 2008). These works look at the architectural typologies that create the urban fabric within the wider territorial framework, but they do not take into account the human component, with mainly an architectural and urban survey.

A second branch is one that looks at and surveys the elements of self-built architectures. In 1936, in Italy, Giuseppe Pagano and Daniel Guarniero already conducted an important study on the origins of Italian rural architecture, analyzing the reasons and logic that determined the characteristics, forms and elements (Pagano and Guarniero, 1936). The work is extensively documented with black and white photographs. In addition to this, Bernard Rudofsky publications, both the 1964, *Architecture without Architects: A Short Introduction to Non-pedigreed Architecture* (Rudofsky, 1987) and the 1977, *The Prodigious Builders: Notes Toward a Natural History of Architecture with Special Regard to those Species that are Traditionally Neglected or Downright Ignored* (Rudofsky, 1979) influenced the research. With his work, Rudofsky highlights the power and importance of un-designed architecture, presenting a worldwide image of non-pedigreed architectures. The 1980 inquiry on popular Portuguese architecture made by the architects' group AAP was also an important reference for this work (AAP, 1980). In this publication, the group of architects surveyed the rural areas of Portugal with a precise collection and recording of the elements of popular Portuguese architecture dispersed across the whole country, both urban and rural. The result was an extensive catalogue made of data and pictures. In this work, the human component is taken into account, as represented within the photo documentation. Also, Cataldi studied and described the spontaneous houses' typologies at a worldwide level, and he stresses that they are organisms that reflect peoples' material and spiritual world, with man's familial microcosmos, social relationships, habits, religious beliefs and activities, and result from long processes of cultural improvements and adaptation to the environment (Cataldi, 2015, p. 9). The works within this branch reinforced the conviction that self-built architecture has to be documented and recorded as an important cultural and physical expression. Finally, as already mentioned, the work of Amos Rapoport was extensively consulted for its approach to spontaneous forms of living, expecially the relation of the house form with culture (Rapoport, 1969, 1988, 1992).

The third area of studies intersected by the research is the one concerning the documentation and survey of self-built architecture both in its formal and informal forms. The 1953 work of Roland Simounet with the group CIAM Alger in the bidonville Mahieddine of Algeri, finalized at the production of a housing project, conceived the inhabitant, the place and the dwelling as indivisible factors. During the preliminary study of the state of facts, Simounet reports these factors in a powerful graphic and photographic synthesis integrating the drawings of house spaces, functions and objects with interviews of the inhabitants (Tesoriere, 2015).

Two previous studies, carried out in Mozambique, were attentively analyzed: the first one by Julio Carrilho on the informal settlements of Lichinga of 2002 (Bruschi, Lage, and Carrilho, 2004), the second by Paul Jenkins on Maputo with the project Homespace of 2012 (Jenkins, 2012).

The architectural survey on the peripheral districts of Lichinga (Niassa Province) made by Julio Carrilho (Bruschi, Lage, and Carrilho, 2004) shows 130 plots in six arranged informal districts. The study demonstrates the importance of the on-site survey to give accurate information on the community use of private and public space. The aim of this study was to give a clear picture of the state of living in Lichinga's informal districts to planners and designers who are going to design the city, and it included architectural elements, spaces and functions and family nucleus main information. The study did not include the analysis of the neighbourhoods' relations.

In Maputo, Paul Jenkins surveyed the home space (defined as the space perceived by the inhabitants as home) in the urban and suburban areas of Maputo, the capital of Mozambique, whose development has similar characteristics to other Sub-Saharan Africa cities (Jenkins, 2012). The Homespace project was conceived as interdisciplinary, including two main areas of knowledge: architecture and planning, and socio-economic and ethnographic. The study focussed on three main facets of the concept of Homespace: the material, the socio-cultural and the political and economic. The unit of analysis in the study is the single household, which is represented in "Life Stories" that link the story of the house with one of its inhabitants. The cells are inserted in the broader context through the social, cultural, political and economic aspects.

Two other international experiences of the survey of informality were taken into consideration: the first one in Hong Kong (SAR, China) and the second one in Sao Paulo (Brazil).

In 2008, the work of Rufina Wu and Stefan Canham documented the Hong Kong rooftop communities, illegal houses standing on top of the metropolis skyscrapers, giving a detailed picture of the living spaces and their inhabitants. The architect Wu, with her surveys and drawings, with the photographer Canham and his photo shoots, went through the documentation of the rooftop housing of five buildings in three neighbourhoods; their work is accompanied by an extensive text by Dr. Ernest Chui, who presents the social and legislative framework in which the rooftop communities are created (Canham and Wu, 2008).

On the other hand, the work in Sao Paulo, carried out in the framework of the PhD of Hugo Mesquita with Christian Kerez, concluded in 2016; it surveyed and reported on selected inner-city favelas in their evolution between 1970 and 2014. The work by Mesquita includes a set of information that integrates the architectural and the urban scale (Mesquita, 2016).

The fourth area intersected by the research regards the studies on Pemba. The two main texts taken into account within this research were the report for the participative project of implementation of the residents' construction skills to face problems related to climate change, made in 2016 by UN Habitat, USAID and the Municipality of Pemba (UN Habitat, USAID, CMCP, 2016), and the PhD thesis *Instrumento de planeamento para cidades médias moçambicanas: o caso de Pemba* carried out at the University of Lisbon by Pereira R. P. S. in 2012 (Pereira, 2012).

The report by the municipality and the two NGOs comprises an on-site survey in five neighbourhoods of Pemba: Paquitequete, Cariacó (Chibuabuari), Josina Machel, Chuiba and Eduardo Mondlane, while the PhD thesis looks at the regional and territorial framing, giving a suggestion of a plan for the reordering of the Paquitequete neighbourhood.

Finally, a wide range of books, papers and articles on the African context, from the socio-economic and urban points of view, and on the history of Mozambique was consulted and is reported in the bibliography. Among these, it is important to mention the anthropological studies of the couple Dias of the 60s and 70s on the Macondes (Dias, 1964/1970) and the book *A short history of Mozambique* by Malyn Newitt (Newitt, 2017) and those of Padraig Carmody *The new scramble for Africa* (Carmody, 2016) and Felwine Sarr's *Afrotopia* (Sarr, 2018) that trace the main lines to tackle the issues related to African socio-economic development and therefore consent to the expansion of the research topics to the urban and dwellings analysis.

The research bridges the gap of knowledge on the current situation of dwellings and settlements in Pemba, analyzing them in four historical phases and at six scales of detail (from the regional framing to the objects), integrating the urban and architectural survey with interviews with inhabitants, graphics and the photographic and aero-photogrammetric tools. This allows for comprehension of the relationships between the interior of the houses and the exterior, in its covered and uncovered spaces, among the inhabitants, the private and the public spaces and their agglomeration in the neighbourhoods. Therefore, the research creates awareness on the current situation of living in Pemba, giving the tools to plan and design the city, taking advantage of the local cultural identity and knowledge of self-building.

Chapters organization

After the premises of the first chapter, used as a general introduction to the research *Spontaneous Living Spaces*, within which the Pemba case study was developed, is the second chapter, which is dedicated to giving an overview of the relevance of Mozambican self-built houses and the reasons for focussing on the city of Pemba. In this chapter, the goals of the research, the methodology used and the main bibliographic references are presented. Chapter 3 is aimed at creating an interpretative framework of Mozambican development regarding what concerns the dwellings and settlements, giving tools to the reader to understand the main historical phases that shaped the development of the country. This is organized in two paragraphs that span from the history and evolution of the Mozambican house to the urbanization trends in Mozambique.

Chapter 4 provides the tools to understand the city of Pemba through the lenses of the research. Three paragraphs frame the case study to let the reader understand from one side the choices made, and from the other the city through an overview at the city scale and an analysis of the aspects that make the urban organism with its localization, climate, history, administrative division, population, urbanization and houses, prevailing economy, infrastructures and social systems. This also addresses the topic of climate extremes, with a specific focus on the two cyclones that, in 2019, deeply injured the country and the Cabo Delgado region.

Chapter 5 is aimed at unpacking the issue of dwellings and settlements in the four selected neighbourhoods, describing in depth the features surveyed on site. Here it is described and shown, with a selection of the graphic and photographic apparatus, the integrated analysis carried out. The chapter starts with an overview of the neighbourhoods and of the blocks surveyed; then it continues with a paragraph on the formation and on the recent evolutions of the neighbourhoods, then focusses on the urban morphological characteristics and then zooms in on the houses with their spaces, functions, elements and objects. The chapter concludes with an analysis of the prevailing types and typologies and with a focus on the new characteristics of living.

In Chapter 6, the conclusions are traced at two different levels: the first embraces the architectural typologies topic which looks at the shift from rural to urban, addressing potentialities and weaknesses of new living spaces. The second level addresses the urban morphology, with a description of the potentialities and weaknesses of the current expansion model and the relationship to new social, cultural, economic and environmental factors.

Notes

1 People living in the neighbourhood are representative of the popular local class. Prevailing occupations are mechanic, farmer, housewife, public employee at the airport or in the municipality, fisherman, workers in the army and so on.
2 According to UN Habitat, the definition of slum is this: "a group of individuals living under the same roof in an urban area who lack one or more of the following: (1) Durable housing of a permanent nature that protects against extreme climate conditions. (2) Sufficient living space which means not more than three people sharing the same room. (3) Easy access to safe water in sufficient amounts at an affordable price. (4) Access to adequate sanitation in the form of a private or public toilet shared by a reasonable number of people (5) Security of tenure that prevents forced evictions". Most of the residential area of Pemba can be considered a slum because of the lack of three (1, 3 and 4) of the aforementioned features.
3 www.ine.gov.moz.

Reference list

Books

AAP. (1980). *Arquitectura Popular em Portugal 4 ed.* Lisboa: Ordem dos Arquitectos.

Abrahamsson, H., and Nilsson, A. (1995). *Mozambique: The Troubled Transition.* London: Zed Books.

Bruschi, S., and Lage, L. (2005). *O Desenho Das Cidades. Moçambique Até O Seculo XXI.* Maputo: FAPF. Faculdade de Arquitectura e Planeamento Físico-UEM, Centro de Estudos e Desenvolvimento do Habitat.

Bruschi, S., Lage, L., and Carrilho, J. (2004). *Traditional Informal Settlements in Mozambique: From Lichinga to Maputo.* Maputo: FAPF. Faculdade de Arquitectura e Planeamento Físico-UEM, Centro de Estudos e Desenvolvimento do Habitat.

Canham, S., and Wu, R. (2008). *Portraits from Above – Hong Kong's Informal Rooftop Communities.* Berlin: Peperoni Books.

Caniggia, G., and Maffei, G. L. (2008). *Lettura dell'edilizia di base.* Firenze: Alinea.

Carmody, P. (2016). *The New Scramble for Africa.* Second Edition. Cambridge: Polity.

Cataldi, G. (2015). *Abitazioni Primitive – Primitive Dwellings.* Firenze: Aión Edizioni.

Conzen, M. R. G. (2012). *L'analisi della forma urbana Alnwick, Northumberland.* Milano: Franco Angeli.

Dias, J. (1964/1970). *Os Macondes de Moçambique,* 4 vols. Lisboa: Junta de Investigação do Ultramar – Centro de Estudos de Antropologia Cultural.

Lévi-Strauss, C. (2017). *L'Antropologia di fronte ai problemi del mondo moderno.* Firenze: Bompiani.

Muratori, S. (1960). *Studi per una Operante Storia Urbana di Venezia*. Roma: Istituto Poligrafico dello Stato.
Newitt, M. (2017). *A Short History of Mozambique*. London: C. Hurst & Co. Ltd.
Pagano, G., and Guarniero, D. (1936). *Architettura Rurale Italiana*. Milano: Ulrico Hoepli.
Pillai, J. (2013). *Cultural Mapping: A Guide to Understanding Place, Community and Continuity. Strategic Information and Research Development Centre*. Selangor: SIRD Strategic Information and Research Development Centre.
Rapoport, A. (1969). *House form and Culture*. Englewood Cliffs, NJ: Prentice-Hall.
Rapoport, A. (1988). *Spontaneous Settlements as Vernacular Design in Patton, C V. (edited by) Spontaneous Shelter – International Perspectives and Prospects*. Philadelphia: Temple University Press.
Rapoport, A. (1992). *On Cultural Landscapes*. in TDSR Vol. III No. II 1992 p. 23–47.
Rudofsky, B. (1979). *The Prodigious Builders*. San Diego: Harcourt Brace Jovanovich.
Rudofsky, B. (1987). *Architecture Without Architects: A Short Introduction to Non-Pedigreed Architecture*. Albuquerque: University of New Mexico Press.
Sarr, F. (2018). *Afrotopia*. Bologna: Edizioni dell'asino.

Documents and reports

Conselho Municipal da Cidade de Pemba. (2014). *Plano Estrategico de Desenvolvimento 2014–2018*.
Jenkins, P. (2012). *Understanding "Home Space" in the African City: A Case Study in Maputo, Mozambique. Synthesis Report*.
ONU. (2015). *World Population Prospect: The 2015 Revision*. New York: ONU.
UN Habitat. (2007). *Relatório sobre o Perfil do Sector Urbano em Moçambique, programa das nações unidas para assentamentos humanos*.
UN Habitat, USAID, Conselho Municipal da Cidade de Pemba. (2016). *Avaliação Rápida da Situação de Infra-estruturas habitacional na Cidade de Pemba no contexto de adaptação as mudanças climáticas Bairros de Paquitequete, Cariacó (Chibuabuari), Josina Machel, Chuiba e Eduardo Mondlane*.

PhD thesis

Mesquita, H. (2016). *Popular Urbanization in São Paulo 1970–2014, A Morphotypological Field Study of Selected Inner-city Squatter Settlements*. PhD ETH Zurich.
Pereira, R. P. S. (2012). *Instrumento de planeamento para cidades médias moçambicanas: o caso de Pemba*. PhD University of Lisbon.

Articles and briefings

Finnegan, W. (1992). *A Complicated War: The Harrowing of Mozambique*. Berkeley: University of California Press.
Lorgen, C. (2000). The Experience of Villagisation: Lessons from Ethiopia, Mozambique, and Tanzania. *Social Dynamics*, Volume 26, pp. 171–198.

Newitt, M. (1995). *A History of Mozambique*. London: Hurst and Company.
Penvenne, J. M. (1998). *Mozambique: a tapestry of conflict in History of Central Africa: The Contemporary Years since 1960*. Ed. David Birmingham and Phyllis Martin. London: Longman. pp 231–266.
Rapoport, A. (1992). On Cultural Landscapes. *Traditional Dwellings and Settlements Review*, Volume 3, No. 2, pp. 33–47.
Tesoriere, Z. (2015). Abitare l'emergenza, L'esperienza maghrebina di Roland Simounet. *Agathón RCAPIA PhD Journal. Recupero dei Contesti Antichi e Processi Innovativi nell'Architettura*. Roma: Aracne. www.academia.edu/10376115/Abitare_l_emergenza._L_esperienza_maghrebina_di_Roland_Simounet
Vines, A. (1991). *Renamo: From Terrorism to Democracy in Mozambique?* London: James Currey.

Websites

Home Space Maputo project | www.homespace.dk
Instituto National de Estatistica | www.ine.gov.moz
UN Development Programme Humand Development Reports | www.hdr.undp.org
UNESCO | www.unesco.org
UN Habitat | www.unhabitat.org
WORLD BANK | www.worldbank.com

3 An interpretative framework of habitation in Mozambique

The origins of the Mozambican house

The origins of the Mozambican house typology reside in the country's history of colonization, firstly by the Swahili and Bantu cultures, up to the 15th century, then by the Portuguese one, from 1505 until 1975, and finally the independence period followed by the civil war and the contemporary and more international phase, from 1992 up to now.

The first one highly impacted the local culture of living; it lasted until the European colonization and was characterized by African internal tribal movements – the Bantu tribes immigration from the northwest of the continent – and then by a Swahili occupation on the coast.

The Swahili are an Arab population of merchants who traded along the Indian Ocean coast, and for this reason their settlements can now be found on the eastern coast of Africa, mainly in Kenya, Tanzania and the northern regions of Mozambique. Swahili merchants used the seasonal monsoon winds to go south in the winter and return north in the summer. Therefore, several strategic ports and villages were settled along the coast. One of these villages was Pemba, the natural port within Pemba Bay.

As Ron van Oers, UNESCO Coordinator for implementation of the 2011 "Recommendation on the Historic Urban Landscape" writes in the *Report on the historic urban landscape workshops and field activities on the Swahili Coast in East Africa 2011–2012*:

> Since the first millennium the Swahili have occupied the nearly 3,000 km long coastline of eastern Africa, a territory which at its greatest extent in the sixteenth century ranged from Mogadishu in Somalia to the South of Mozambique. As one of several mercantile societies located around the rim of the Indian Ocean, they mastered long-distance seafaring with the use of the monsoon wind system to conduct trade across the ocean.

For over 1,000 years the Swahili constructed and maintained a literate society, based on Islam, and a commercial empire founded on intercontinental trade and plantation agriculture.

(UNESCO, 2013, p. 6)

According to the aforementioned UNESCO report on the Swahili Historic Urban Landscape, the physical foundation of Swahili society and civilization is urban, and a mixture of cultural and architectural influences characterizes Swahili towns. This created and inhabited a "system of island archipelagos and mainland port cities bound by language, colonialism, and monsoon trade winds" (UNESCO, 2013, p. 6). The multiculturality of this system created a dynamic urbanism that reflected the influence of this global network. According to Joseph Heathcott in the previously cited UNESCO report, the elements of the Swahili city are mainly (1) the market, (2) the interstitial space, (3) the public spaces, (4) the expansion spaces and (5) the template spaces (UNESCO, 2013).

Looking at the scale of architecture, the concept of house is characterized by a sequence of open and closed spaces in which constructions can function as shelters or for storage. Being in a polygamous society, it happens that multiple wives might live in the same plot/house and share common spaces and activities. Therefore, it is possible that more than one family lives in a house which traditionally belongs to the same family nucleus. In this house concept, covered spaces usually consist of huts, and each family member has use of one hut of the house with the exception of children under the age of 14, who live with women. Trees are always present in the courtyard as they provide shade and fruits, and they used to be considered sacred elements of the house.

According to Sandro Bruschi in *Era Uma Vez Uma Palhota* (Bruschi, Lage, and Carrilho, 2005), the traditional house typology in southern Africa was characterized by an articulation of open and closed spaces, where different quarters were positioned around a circular shape, with a hierarchical order. The quarters were then built in cylindrical shapes with conical roofs.

This is the enlarged family house (called *muti*) of many of the southern native populations (such as the Thonga, the Maconde, the Bantu and so on), and it was designed following the circular symbolic shape of divinity and life. Because of its circularity, it was more difficult to aggregate one with another, and therefore, it is a house type that could not easily evolve in agglomerations.

The northern area of Mozambique – where the case study is located – is an exception to this typology as, from the second half of the 19th century, it was influenced by the Swahili culture presenting a rectangular typology with a saddle or hipped roof that, especially in the regions inhabited by the Yao, Macua and Makonde people, replaced the circular native types

(Bruschi, Lage, and Carrilho, 2004). This rectangular house type allowed the aggregation in settlements by alignment in a grid of streets.

> The old Swahili cities that existed outside the political frontiers of pres-ent Mozambique, from Somalia up to Tanzania, have left evidence of a rather elaborate architecture. The buildings, of several floors, had cupolas and stone and lime walls, using coral rock as building mate-rial. In the Swahili settlements found along the Mozambican coast, it is only in some rare cases that remains of stone buildings preced-ing the Portuguese conquest have been found (Duarte, 1993). In other cases, the absence of significant, archaeological remains questions the existence of real cities (Duarte and Meneses, 1996), even though some authors solely attribute this absence to the difficulty in finding lasting construction materials in this region (Newitt, 1997, p. 31). At present, it is thought that Swahili urban civilization consisted of a hierarchy of centres and that only the affluent peoples lived in stone buildings. In some cases, the presence of dwellings, within the same settlements but of different construction techniques (made out of coral stones with cupolas or flat roofs, consisting of palm posts structure covered with mats made of palm leaves with saddle roof, or using wattle and daub with thatched roof), confirms that the use of different materials did not correspond to the availability of natural resources, but to different economic levels (Kusimba, 1999, pp. 149–152).
>
> (Bruschi, Lage, and Carrilho, 2004, p. 48)

Swahili types of houses with hipped roofs are present today in Pemba, as reported in the integrated on-site analysis.

Concerning the building techniques, Bruschi reports that most of the southern African houses are made with wattle and daub and

> in most cases the walls are made of a thick interlacement filled with small stones and a clay paste. The roof is with palm fronds or straw arranged on bamboo. All the construction is built on high clay, stone base or on a platform. The roof structure, which is a hipped roof, is characterized by two posts that are higher than the walls to support the ridge beam. The rafters, secured at the ridge, are fanned-out being fixed on a beam that goes all around the house. As with the conical roof, the fan-shaped roof, guarantees the uniform distribution of static stress on the structure.
>
> (Bruschi, Lage, and Carrilho, 2004, p. 49)

The veranda is an important architectural element of this house typology that was imported in the Swahili type from the circular one. It is present all around the conical roof of the circular type, and in the Swahili house, it was applied on the two longer sides or on the four sides of the rectangular plan. This architectural element provides shade and protection and allows for the maintenance of better climatic conditions within the house, and at the same time, it creates a filter between the open and the closed spaces (Bruschi, Lage, and Carrilho, 2004).

The Swahili type, used in denser areas, in time was influenced both by the circular typology and the Portuguese one. In fact, if most of the African houses remained in isolated settlements with a hardly noticeable entrance, the modern Swahili house type is used in urban settlements. The typology is repeated, aligned to the street front, and, through its conformation, it is able to connect the public (street) to the private space (house building and courtyard), with the house entrance directly from the street. This connection spreads to the inner courtyard through the central corridor that connects the main entrance to the backyard and that distributes the rooms on its two sides. The rectangular plan of the house is reflected also in the rectangular shape of the plot, where most of the living activities are performed (such as the living room, the kitchen, the bathroom, the latrine and the extra quarters). This 90° angular plan of the house, comprising built-up and open inner spaces, allows for the organization of the settlements within the urban fabric (Bruschi, Lage, and Carrilho, 2004).

Furthermore, the openings, both on the street side and on the courtyard side, are symmetrical. On the central axis is the door, giving access to the corridor, flanked on the left and right sides with windows.

During the colonial period, the Swahili typology was kept in its main features of the rectangular plan, with the corridor distribution, the hipped roof, the relationship (through the veranda) to the street with the courtyard and the symmetry of the openings. However, three main factors determined the evolution of the typology: (1) the increase in dimensions, (2) the introduction of baked bricks for the walls and metal sheets for the roof and (3) the substitution of the wooden poles of the veranda with brick pillars (Bruschi, Lage, and Carrilho, 2004).

Since independence, the Swahili house typology did not have massive changes, and, in the contemporary context of extremely rapid growth, the rectangular house with a hipped roof is still present. However, according to Bruschi, and to the surveys in his studies, this typology is probably destined to disappear because of the introduction of new technologies that are cheaper and easily replaceable. For example, the introduction of the metal sheets for the roof threatens the traditional internal distribution of the house, as the metallic roof is independent from the house structure, and therefore, they do not need to be related. Furthermore, the speed in urbanization is affecting the number of inhabitants of each unit and, as a consequence, the number of rooms or the number of quarters within the plot need to be augmented. Self-building, for the low- and medium-income living typology, still prevails.

Outlining the urbanization trends in the history of Mozambique: from a rural to an urban society

According to the majority of published information on the topic, in Mozambique, the European conception of urban form did not exist before the Swahili and the Portuguese colonization. Historically and archaeologically, it is not possible to find relevant information since the sources are limited to the last 500 years of colonization. The existing episodes of urbanization were exceptions to the rural environment and were mainly centralizing those classes that had the commercial and/or combative power. The natives and lower classes were living and working in enlarged family settlements in the rural area. Therefore, there were two patterns of living that parallelly coexisted: the family village scattered in the territory and the colonial settlements along the coast, and this trend is still visible in the country (Bruschi and Lage, 2005).

Bruschi, Lage and Carrilho give a general overview of the native settlements in Ancient Africa in *Era Uma Vez Uma Palhota* (Bruschi, Lage, and Carrilho, 2005), where the settlements up to the 15th century and from the 19th century are described. In this publication, Bruschi writes that, in the Ancient Africa of the 15th century, two kinds of settlements could be found. First, north of the Zambezi River, the Great Zimbabwe, which was composed of migrant settlements that changed locations any time that the resources of the territory became scarce, or because of the chief's death or due to fights with other tribes. Since the 12th century, the Zimbabwe population inhabited the settlements of the interior of the country, mainly between the Zambezi and Limpopo rivers (in between what is now called Mozambique and Zimbabwe). These villages were characterized by circular walls in stone that separated the houses of the dominant from those of the lower class of the population. Houses were built in clay and vegetal materials. In the middle of the 15th century, with the decline of commerce, these settlements were abandoned. Afterwards, villages in Mozambique were mainly temporary and served only for defence. With the arrival of colonizers, these settlements were seen – after a short time of excitement by the explorers of the native cities – as 'miserable' aggregations of huts.

The second type of settlement was characterized by the Islamic influence, and it was seen all along the eastern coastline of Africa. On the northern coast, the settlements stood along the routes of Berbers' caravans, while on the south they were mainly Swahili. These were stable settlements that stood on key points for navigation and for exchanging goods. The Swahili arrived on the Mozambican coast during the 14th century, and the Portuguese documented that at their arrival, there was a series of Swahili ports and settlements along the coast. During the Swahili colonization, the most important commercial settlement was Sofala, which was strategic for trading with Arabia and the Orient. Among the settlements of the south, the most important were Quiloane and the archipelago of Bazaruto, while in the northern areas, Quelimane and Quiloa (today Kilwa, Tanzania) and then a number of smaller centres such as Angoche, the Island of Mozambique, Caboceira, Somana, the Ibo Island and Pemba arose. The Swahili urban system was characterized by an internal network of points of exchange, ruled by local powers, for trading the most interesting goods such as gold and ivory. Swahili settlements were usually made up of multi-storey architectures in coral stone with a certain degree of prestige. However, in the Mozambican area, traces of these settlements are lacking, probably due to the scarcity of long-lasting construction materials on site (Bruschi and Lage, 2005).

Along the coast, as the Portuguese colonizers arrived, they destroyed almost all of the Swahili settlements and occupied and fortified some of them, such as Sofala (1505), the Island of Mozambique (1507), Quelimane (1540) and Ibo Island (after the 1522). The colonists were not able to conquer the interior settlements. These settlements, however, lost their main commercial activity and were gradually abandoned. The Portuguese were able to penetrate the interior of the country just in the 18th century and created the fortified settlements of Zumbo (1715) and Manica (1720).

During the 19th century, the main urban design activity implemented by the Portuguese in the Mozambican cities followed the Roman military grid of the *castrum*. The grid was made of equally large streets that created compact blocks divided into plots that at that time were usually rectangular. A central block hosted the main square and the representative buildings. In the years 1945–1955, a phase of "formal urbanism" was carried out thanks to the start of the activity of the *Gabinete de Urbanização Colonial*, an office dependent on the Ministry of Colonies that controlled the plans' production and design for the following decade. These plans emphasized the central areas of cities through the use of perspective visual elements, such as main axes converting on the squares. The central areas were used for monumental exhibitions of Portuguese power. The plans, created in this period for Maputo and Beira city, are still an important tool for the actual town planning. The last 15 years of occupation, from 1960 until 1975, were characterized by the rationalist movement. The planning activity was given to the *Secção de Urbanização de Moçambique* and to the *Direcção das Obras Públicas e Comunicações do Ministério do Ultramar* and then (in 1964) to the *Repartição de Urbanismo da Direcção Provincial dos Serviços de Obras Públicas e Transportes de Moçambique*. Functionality was the new main requirement of the plans that were designed in these years. The production was intense, with several plans for the majority of the main cities.

It is important to underline that, in all these centuries of urban development, the local population was not really taken into account in the urban design and planning. Some of the plans started to include areas for the local people just in the late colonial period, and they were always located on the peripheries. The local population was living, or on the edges, of the colonial city or in rural areas, in their traditional way of living. It is just after independence that a proper form of urbanization with services and infrastructures for the native population was taken into consideration.

Parallel to the Portuguese cities' evolution, Mozambican settlements disappeared until the 19th century, when in the south, the Gaza reign (province of Gaza) became an important centre of power. However, the reign's settlement was not very relevant for its architecture as it consisted in a surrounding defensive wall, in poles and mud, which protected the house of the chief and of his court. At the same time, in the northern regions, the Yao population created an important network of local reigns based on slave commerce. Among these, the most important and recorded settlement was the Mwembe by I Nyambi Mataka.[1] In 1866, the explorer David Livingstone described Mwembe as an extended and well-organized settlement with houses and farms, and he counted 1000 residential units, mainly of the Swahili type, and, in 1889, the bishop Johnson documented that 5000 houses were in the settlement (Bruschi and Lage, 2005, p. 14).

Up to the 19th century, Mozambican cities were characterized by a duality: the *cidade de cimento*, the area where Portuguese worked and lived, and the *cidade de canniço*, the area where indigenous people lived. This distinction was evident in the *Indigenato policy*: a policy in effect until 1962 and based on the division of the population into civilized and indigenous peoples. From 1975, after independence, new forms of class-based differentiation were implemented as at the end of the colonial regime, most of the Portuguese colonial population (approximately 190,000 people) left the country, and the postcolonial FRELIMO government initiated the nationalization of the abandoned urban estate properties. All the land became public property, and the new governance structure of neighbourhoods (called *bairros*) began its implementation. The land use right, delimited on the surface of land and the corresponding airspace, is granted with the DUAT (*Direito de Uso e Aproveitamento da Terra*)[2] for 99 years. With the 2007 land law, the DUAT was confirmed, reaffirming that any citizen who could demonstrate a ten-year occupancy had the right to occupy the land (bona fide right).[3]

The early years of independence (gained on June 25th, 1975) characterized the urban fabric of most of the Mozambican cities as we know them today. In fact, as in most of the African socialist countries (see the experience of Ujiama in Tanzania), the newly born governing party FRELIMO imposed the grouping of the houses with a Villagization Policy to control and activate the population that was living in enlarged family houses scattered in the territory. After independence, the country needed to rebuild its social, economic and cultural systems while facing an internal war between FRELIMO and RENAMO (the opposition party) that lasted until 1992 when the peace agreements were made (*Accordi di pace di Roma*). During the villagization process, the government first invited and then forced people to move and build their own houses in cities, following urban schemes, imposed by the authorities who were including the basic infrastructures. During the years between 1975 and 1985, an intensive planning activity designed most of the Mozambican cities around the colonial settlements. Cities were ordered, and during the urbanization process, rural typologies were brought and adapted to the urban environment. The main designers of these operations were first the *Direcção National da Habitação* and then the *Serviços Provinciais de Planeamento Físico*. This process involved the entire population, and the logistical conditions were difficult (Forjaz, 1987, pp. 47–65).

The new administrative organization is characterized by six territorial administrative units: (1) the province, managed by the Provincial Governor, (2) the city, managed by the city executive council and the city assembly, (3) the urban district, managed by the administrator, (4) the communal neighbourhoods (*bairros communais*), managed by the director of communal neighbourhoods, (5) the *quartierão*, block of 50 to 100 houses, managed by the chief of *quartierão* and (6) the *dez casas* (ten households), managed by its chief.

In the 1980s, the first National Urban Planning Meeting defined the priority of interventions required for the 12 provinces in the country so that an urban and territorial planning system was organized. The *Instituto Nacional de Planeamento Físico* (INPF)[4] was established and focussed on the need to prepare the *Planos Físicos e Planos de Intervenções Prioritários*.[5]

The planning activity was structured enough to permit foreign consultants to prepare plans together with the *Serviços Provinciais de Planeamento Físico*. Among the new plans was the *Projecto de conjunto residencial para a Presidência da República em Pemba e proposta para o desenvolvimento turístico da praia de Wimbi*. This plan, created for the development of a residential area and a touristic one in the Wimbi area of Pemba, was designed by a group of Mexican consultants in the years 1975–1982 (Bruschi and Lage, 2005, p. 66). In this type of urban fabric, with rectangular and aligned plots, the evolution of Swahili houses typology, as seen before, was easily implementable.

Today Mozambique faces important economic growth, expecting an increase in jobs and wealth with the production of liquid gas and tourism. This upsurge has led to the creation of employment in the urban environment. Consequently, the building capacity and the possibility of expenses in the dwelling sector is growing.

At the beginning of the 21st century, 80% of the urban population in Mozambique was living in informal settlements, as self-built houses did not have the basic infrastructures. In fact, municipalities are not able to make economic investments to relocate or to offer better living conditions to their inhabitants.

Therefore, the process of development that is in progress is considering different actors, among which are the municipalities, the inhabitants (and builders) and, in some cases, international organizations.

The positive aspect of this general lack of infrastructures and organization, is that Mozambican cities have the possibility to experiment with a new social and spatial organization that can create new forms of urbanization. Work and lifestyles are changing and are fostering the urbanization process, and the population is rapidly growing.

Notes

1 I Nyambi Mataka was an important Yao trader who founded his reign that flourished because of slaves and ivory trade.
2 Right of use and benefit of the land.
3 The Mozambican land management system can be divided into four levels, from the national and provincial to the district and municipal level. There are two main instruments of the national management: (1) the National Plan for Territorial Development (*Plano Nacional de Desenvolvimento Territorial* – PNDT) and (2) in which are highlighted the perspectives and the general guidelines for the whole national territory and the intervention priorities and the Special Plans for Spatial Planning (*Planos Especiais de Ordenamento do Território* – PEOT), which define use parameters and conditions for interprovincial zones. According to the provincial management, the Provincial and Interprovincial Territorial Development Plans (*Planos Provinciais de Desenvolvimento Territorial* – PPDT) can be found which organize one or more provinces and define the guidelines, measures and actions necessary for the development of the territory. At the district level, the main instrument is the District and Inter-District Land Use Plans (*Planos Distritais de Uso da Terra* – PD), while the municipal management system is articulated in three main planning tools: (1) the Urban Structure Plans (*Planos de Estrutura Urbana* – PE), which draws the municipal spatial organization and defines the related parameters and rules; (2) the General Urban Planning Plans (*Planos Gerais de Urbanização* – PGU) and Partial Urbanization Plans (*Planos Parciais de Urbanização* – PPUs) and (3) the Detailed Plans (*Planos de Pormenor* – PP).
4 National Institute for the Physical Planning.

5 Physical Plans and Priority Intervention Plans. These were followed in particular with the 1998 *Lei de Bases da Política do Ordenamento do Território e do Urbanismo Português* and the 2007 *Política de Ordenamento do Território*.

Reference list

Bruschi, S., and Lage, L. (2005). *O Desenho Das Cidades. Moçambique Até O Seculo XXI*. Maputo: FAPF. Faculdade de Arquitectura e Planeamento Físico-UEM, Centro de Estudos e Desenvolvimento do Habitat.

Bruschi, S., Lage, L., and Carrilho, J. (2004). *Traditional Informal Settlements in Mozambique: From Lichinga to Maputo*. Maputo: FAPF. Faculdade de Arquitectura e Planeamento Físico-UEM, Centro de Estudos e Desenvolvimento do Habitat.

Bruschi, S., Lage, L., and Carrilho, J. (2005). *Era Uma Vez Uma Palhota*. Maputo: FAPF. Faculdade de Arquitectura e Planeamento Físico-UEM, Centro de Estudos e Desenvolvimento do Habitat.

Duarte, R. T. (1993). *Northern Mozambique in the Swahili World*. An archaeological approach. Uppsala: Uppsala University – Department of Archaeology.

Duarte, R. T., Meneses, M. P. (1996). *The Archaeology of Mozambique Islands*, in Pwiti Gilbert, Soper Robert (eds.), Aspects of African Archaeology – Papers from the 10th Congress of the Pan African Association for Prehistory and Related Studies, Harare: University of Zimbabwe Publications, pp. 555–560.

Forjaz, J. (1987). La Pianificazione fisica nel Mozambico indipendente. In Ferracuti Gianni (ed.), *Da Lourenço Marques a Maputo. La riconversione della città coloniale tra ideologia e politiche urbane*. Milano: Franco Angeli, pp. 47–65.

Kusimba, C. M. (1999). *The Rise and Fall of Swahili State*, Walnut Creek: Altamira Press.

Newitt, M. (1997). History of Mozambique, C. London: Hurst and Co., 1995 (ed. port. História de Moçambique, Publicações Europa-America, Mem Martins).

UNESCO. (2013). Swahili Historic Urban Landscapes, report on the historic urban landscape workshops and field activities on the Swahili coast in East Africa 2011–2012. Paris: UNESCO.

4   Understanding Pemba

An integrated analysis

In the framework of the *Spontaneous Living Spaces* research project, spontaneous living is considered a fundamental element of the urban landscape and of the heritage of a place, both in its tangible and intangible forms. Therefore, its documentation and understanding, in order to preserve, communicate and enhance the diversity of the cultural expressions, is of fundamental importance.

Pemba is studied through an integrated analysis of its characteristics of living regarding what concerns its residential self-built architecture present in selected neighbourhoods. Understanding the building techniques implemented, the distribution of spaces and functions and the relationships between the private and public dimensions and among different levels of openness of the living spaces allows us to acquire an awareness of the living style and the trends of change.

The 50 dwellings and four settlements surveyed were analyzed according to several scales of detail: the objects, houses' spaces and functions (1:200), the houses agglomerations within the blocks (1:500), the neighbourhoods (1:1000) and the regional analysis (1:5000). Furthermore, the PEUM (*Plano de Estruttura Urbana Municipal*) was studied and analyzed in all parts of the survey, diagnosis, and vision to make the bigger picture clear. The analysis led to the determination of the houses' typologies in the four neighbourhoods. These typologies were then confronted with the Mozambican Swahili house type, detecting the characteristics of variance and permanence.

The integrated analysis was developed through three phases: (1) the preliminary documentation, (2) the on-site survey and (3) the representation and interpretation.

The preliminary documentation phase was needed for understanding the Mozambican context (from the historical, geographical and social points of view), the evolution of the city of Pemba and the prevailing housing typology and history at the national scale. The on-site phase of the survey was carried out in Pemba in July 2016. As the survey was aimed at understanding the characteristics of living in a stable condition and not the types of emergencies or risks, the selected period corresponded to the dry season in order to facilitate the on-site operations. In addition, the selected neighbourhoods are not considerable informal; instead they are part of the formal urban fabric, and they represent four periods of expansion of the city which were built in four different historical phases.

City scale overview

Pemba is an intermediate Mozambican city located on the coast in the far north of the country and is the capital of the Cabo Delgado region. It was born as a Swahili port settlement, precisely because of its location on the Pemba Bay, which makes it a perfect natural port that later was used also by the Europeans during the centuries of Portuguese colonization. The city is characterized by exceptional natural and landscape resources, such as kilometres of white beaches with lively coral reefs, and it is the gateway for the Quirimbas Archipelago, a natural park which, since 2018, is registered as a biosphere reserve on the UNESCO World Heritage List.

Pemba is limited in size, but it is experiencing a strong population increase. Precisely for these two reasons, combined with the historicity of its development, it represents an ideal case study both to observe the evolution of the Mozambican culture of living and to imagine alternative development dynamics that place the relationship between man and the environment at the centre.

As previously mentioned, the regional analysis was investigated through a 1:5000 scale with maps aimed at creating the framework to understand the dynamics of settling, mobility and of living. The layers used for the analysis were the (1) elevation, (2) the broad-crowned vegetation, (3) the neighbourhoods and morphology of the city, (4) the infrastructures combined with the soil elevation and (5) the city historical phases evolution. These layers were then superposed to analyze their interaction. This part of the analysis was mainly done during the preliminary documentation and then confirmed or, when needed, corrected during the on-site survey.

The city rises from sea level up to 108 metres. The airport and the main street are located on its ridge. The main infrastructures are the port, the airport and five built-up *avenidas*, with the project of expansion of the Avenida da Marginal along the eastern coast. The great majority of the other streets are unpaved.

The popular neighbourhoods are settled mainly along the beaches and escarpment, and from a morphological point of view, in some cases they follow a matrix grid organization, while in other cases they are organized by following the topographical contour lines.

The city finds its origins in the Paquitequete neighbourhood, where the Swahili settlement was, and then it expanded in the colonial period. Since independence, the evolution was concentrated in grid settlements along the main infrastructures. The contemporary expansion is more informal and reaches further areas such as Chuiba, Mahate and Muxara. A rich vegetation characterizes the city, mainly with broad-crowned trees, used by dwellers for shade and for productive purposes.

Recently, the municipality created the PEUM, a plan for Pemba with a vision that should have been implemented in the years 2014–2018. The vision implementation is ongoing and is focussed on the expansion of several sectors, such as residential, agricultural, industrial, infrastructural and touristic. A relevant change is the ongoing one in the Chuiba neighbourhood, which represents an area of expansion for touristic activity.

Framing the Pemba case study

Localization

Pemba is the capital of the Province of Cabo Delgado, the northeast region of Mozambique bordering Tanzania. It is located in a bay named Pemba. Pemba Bay is ranked third in the world based on its size, trailing after Guanabara Bay in Brazil and Sidney Bay in Australia, and it hosts the Pemba commercial harbour. The city is 194 km², and it is considered the main political, administrative, infrastructural, industrial, commercial, cultural and touristic pole of the region (Conselho Municipal da Cidade de Pemba, 2014). Its coordinates are 10° 29' north, 14° 01' south latitude and 35° 58' west, 40° 35' east longitude. Pemba city borders Metuge District on the north and east and Mecufi District on the south. Its eastern border is characterized by 30 km of coastline along the Indian Ocean. An overview of the city's elevation, neighbourhoods and infrastructures is given by the map of Figure 4.1.

The population belongs to different ethnic groups. The prevailing social groups speak several languages, among them the most popular are the Macua, Maconde, Mwanì, Swahili, Portuguese, English and French languages. The prevailing religions are Muslim, Catholic and Protestant (Data INE – Delegação de Cabo Delgado – Pemba).

Climate

In general terms, because it is located in the Capricorn tropical zone, Pemba has a humid tropical climate. Tracing an overview of its characteristics, the monsoonal regime creates two distinct seasons: wet and dry, and the rain distribution is irregular throughout the year. During the hot season, from December to April, the average temperature varies from 25°C to 37°C, with

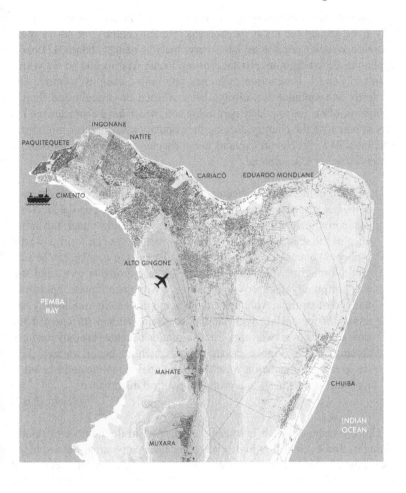

Figure 4.1 Map of Pemba's elevation, neighbourhoods and infrastructures
Source: Corinna Del Bianco

rainfalls reaching between 800mm and 1000mm and with relative humidity falling between 80% and 90%.

However, climate extremes have hit African territories hard. The Western world has recently begun to experience them, but still, for it, climate extremes are abstract themes because they are still far from people's everyday lives, except for minor phenomena. On the contrary, in Africa these extreme weather conditions have very specific names: famines, floods, typhoons, desertification, coastal erosion, locust swarms and so on, which result in hunger, destruction of houses and crops, inability to move and so forth. Mozambique has always been affected by drought and famine problems, often due to poorly permeable soil, which have characterized the development of the country, forcing the population to continue migrations (Newitt, 2017). As Newitt explains in the chapter on climate in her book, *A short history of Mozambique*:

> Rainfall in the south is irregular and this factor, coupled with the poor soils, has resulted in much of the south being thinly populated. North of approximately latitude 24 south, the land falls under the influence of the seasonal monsoon winds (which at sea can form powerful typhoons) but even here rains are irregular and the country can be subject to droughts which may last years. These droughts were, and still are, profoundly disruptive and can bring with them famine, epidemics and locust swarms. Although rural communities have traditionally had strategies for dealing with famine, these are seldom sufficient if the drought lasts over two years. Then migration becomes the only recourse forcing people to move towards areas which are better watered. This has created a population which is used to being mobile and has led to migrations, conquests and profound political disturbance.
>
> (Newitt, 2017)

Climate change, which is causing an increase in the number of floods, droughts and cyclones, is highly affecting the Pemba area. For example, over time several cyclones have damaged the city. The oldest documented storm was in 1904, followed by one in 1914 that destroyed most of the houses, then one in 1987, and finally, in 2019 the two cyclones Idai and Kenneth, and in this regard, it is appropriate to open a parenthesis.

Many of the houses that were taken over, in their simplicity and their ephemeral characteristic, in 2019 were destroyed, uncovered and flooded by the two violent cyclones that hit East Africa and in particular Mozambique.

The first cyclone, Idai, hit in March, in particular in the Beira area, while the second, Kenneth, hit in April in the coastal area to the north, in particular the Isle of Ibo and the region of Cabo Delgado, including Pemba. Idai was particularly destructive, falling on the city of Beira, the capital of the Sofala province and the second largest city in Mozambique. It involved around 8,500,000 people, including around 146,000 who were relocated and more than 500 who were killed, in addition to the thousands injured. Hospitals were partially or completely damaged, suffering the loss of equipment, medicines and health products (Pozniak, 2020). Kenneth, a Category 3 cyclone on the Saffir-Simpson scale, on the other hand, crashed on April 25, 2019, on the north coast of Mozambique and is the strongest tropical cyclone ever recorded on the African continent, characterized by strong winds with peaks up to 220 km/h and incessant rain (Cambaza, 2019). The cyclone caused at least 45 deaths and destroyed around 40,000 homes, leaving 374,000 people in need of assistance. The cyclone destroyed health infrastructures, including the existing small sewerage system, toilets and latrines, and water collection systems, creating a strong risk of developing waterborne epidemics. As already mentioned, the city of Pemba, periodically, with the rainy season, is an area where cholera is endemic. Following the cyclone, the risk of cholera-related episodes becoming an epidemic (in the coastal and non-insular area) was very high. A week after the cyclone in Pemba and Mecufi, there were 14 cases of cholera, and 10 days later they had risen to 149. As reported by Cambaza, the response from the government and partners was exceptional, also taking into account the plan adopted in response to the spread of cholera (Cholera Response Plan for Beira) on the occasion of the cyclone Idai hitting Beira. The response included prevention campaigns, the creation of treatment centres and a coordination project for the improvement of water, health and hygiene (Cambaza, 2019). Even the islands of the Quirimbas Archipelago were severely hit. The Italian NGO Oikos, which was working in response to the emergency, reported that 95% of the population in Ibo had been left homeless, and public facilities such as hospitals and primary schools were seriously damaged.[1] In addition, due to the strong winds and heavy rains, rescue operations by helicopter, on foot or by road were only able to take place when the weather subsided, after several days, and even then the roads were completely flooded and impassable. People were left without food, and a population that practices subsistence agriculture in house courtyards were obviously left with nothing. In addition, even the resource of fishing was affected: the boats were destroyed and had to be repaired, the rains made the sea difficult to sail, and finally, the fish, of which the Indian Ocean is generally rich, had swam away from the coasts.

The country, already very humbled, literally found itself on its knees.

In February 2020, as a result of the copious rains of the previous seasons, an invasion of locusts broke out all over East Africa, devastating Somalia, then Ethiopia, Kenya and Congo. The correlation between events is attributable to man's lack of ability to regulate the dynamics between various elements and is manifested precisely in a context in which human beings' relationship with the environment and with other species is particularly strong. In 2019, there were not only cyclones but also drought and then floods, which provide clear evidence of what the climate emergency means and Mozambique represents as one of the most vulnerable and least pre-pared countries to deal with disasters. In addition, to combat the emergency, the Mozambican government had to ask for further loans, which will slow down its development even more. (COSACA, 2019)

The populations find themselves having to battle the issue of climate extremes, starting from self-built houses that characterize the neighbour-hoods of African cities. These houses are very simple and are not able to structurally resist the weather, particularly violent climatic episodes.

Various projects have been undertaken to try to help the population increase the structural resistance of housing with a bottom-up process; for example, in Pemba, the UN Habitat and USAID project, with the municipal-ity, aimed precisely at improving the building capacity of the inhabitants to resist atmospheric threats brought about by climate change, such as floods, cyclones and erosion (UN Habitat, USAID, CMCP, 2016). However, the project was suspended by the Trump government.

Self-construction, in these situations, was a weakness on the one hand but a strength on the other, as the inhabitants were able to rebuild their homes, and with the help of international rescue projects, the infrastruc-tures, schools and hospitals have been brought back into operation.

Origins

The bay is supposedly of volcanic origin, as an abundance of pumice stone characteristic of vulcanized rock was found. The assumption, however, is contradicted by its constitution, which is calcareous and not basalt.

The bay has always represented a natural safe port. In fact, the stories on its origins are related to this peculiarity. There are two primary stories that narrate the birth of the settlement. The first tells of a lady who survived a shipwreck, settled in Paquitequete and was then followed by fishermen who settled in the same neighbourhood, which allowed easy access to the sea. The second ver-sion of the story of the birth of the city narrates that a group of indigenous per-sons who were coming from Zanzibar were transported by a European, landed in the bay and were attacked by flies. They started screaming "Pembe!" which means fly in Swahili. From that episode Pemba was named.

The city developed as a port city during the Swahili occupation and then during the Portuguese occupation.

In the period from 1850–1975, Pemba faced consistent changes. In fact, it was considered a village in 1889, then a small town in 1934 and finally a city in 1958. The plans that accompanied this development were:

1   *Planta de Porto Amélia* (expansion project) dated 1921 (Silveira, s. d., vol. 2, est. 463);

2   *Planta da povoação de Porto Amélia* (expansion project) dated 1936
    (*Centro de Documentação* MICOA);
3   *Foral* approved with the *Diploma legislativo* n° 862 dated July 31,
    1943;
4   *Ante-plano Geral de Urbanização* (preliminary urban plan) dated
    1950, João Aguiar – *Gabinete de Urbanização Colonial* (*Centro de
    Documentação* – MICOA; AHM, D.21.2);
5   *Plano de Urbanização* (urbanization plan) datable from 1961 to
    1963, Paulo de Melo Sampaio; (*Centro de Documentação* – MICOA)
    approved with order of August 2, 1965;
6   *Planos Parciais* (partial plans) approved with ordinance n° 19,909 pub-
    lished in B.O. of January 21, 1967.

Administrative division and population

Pemba municipality is composed of ten neighbourhoods represented by
administrative divisions. These are: Alto Gingone, Cariacó, Cimento,
Chuiba, Eduardo Mondlane, Ingonane, Mahate, Muxara, Natite and Paquitequete. After Cariacó, Natite is the most populated neighbourhood, followed by Alto Gingone and Paquitequete. Since 2007, they have been
growing proportionally.

The table 4.1 shows the growth of the population per division with the
data of the *Instituto Nacional de Estatística*, of the 2007 and 2014 census,
with the neighbourhoods analyzed in the case study highlighted.

Table 4.1 Number of inhabitants per neighbourhood and their area in 2014. Data
PEUM

	Administrative division	*2007 n. of inhabitants*	*2014 n. of inhabitants*	*Area (hectares)*
1	Alto Gingone	14,993	23,989	769
2	Cariacó	46,562	53,546	589
3	Cimento	4,304	7,532	297
4	Chuiba	4,238	7,417	2,045
5	Eduardo Mondlane	10,485	23,591	1,524
6	Ingonane	13,738	18,546	86
7	Mahate	5,400	12,150	1,179
8	Muxara	5,872	13,212	3,175
9	Natite	22,800	30,780	152
10	Paquitequete	13,314	16,643	81
Total		**141,706**	**190,763**	

Urbanization and houses

A grid of the main and secondary streets, in which rectangular plots are located, characterizes the settlements. Usually each family occupies one plot. The land is owned by the State, and its use is controlled with long-term rents regulated by the DUAT.[2] However, informal settlements are present in several neighbourhoods of the city. Cariacó and Paquitequete are the most critical ones, where informality is accompanied by problems like erosion and the lack of streets, water, electricity and other public services. Informality is present also in some areas of Eduardo Mondlane, Chuiba, Mahate, Alto Gingone and Muxara and in the area in between the port and the airport.

The city grew consistently in the last decade, and the PEDM explains that there are four main reasons for this growth: (1) the rural exodus – Pemba represents an increase of the working and living conditions being the main urban centre of the Cabo Delgado region; (2) the legal and illegal immigration from Tanzania; (3); the exploration and extraction of natural resources both from national and international businesses; (4) the civil war – which led people to move to bigger urban centres to find security. People coming into the city for this reason usually hurried to build their houses, often settling in areas dedicated to the construction of infrastructures (like streets, schools, hospitals and so on), giving origin to informal areas.

Furthermore, the PEDM highlights the five main problems that are affecting the city, such as (1) the lack of streets in the neighbourhoods; (2) the lack of territorial planning; (3) the lack of a politic providing housing to young people; (4) the lack of a structural plan and; (5) the lack of opportunities for low-cost housing, especially for young people and for the unemployed.

Economy

The economy of the city is composed of sectors that historically involve both locals and foreigners. Commerce and tourism-related services (hotels, restaurants and bars, travel agencies and so on) represent the most relevant sector (commerce with 40% of activities and tourism with more than the 20%) and are accompanied by public functions that have the highest number of employed, followed by industry, education, agriculture and other minor activities.

One-third of the total population is practicing subsistence farming along the green belt of the city. This provides, to the majority of the families, higher food security and, in some cases, money to buy other goods and/or services. The main crops cultivated in the Pemba area are the manioc, maize, vegetables, fruit, cowpea and millet. Traditionally, agricultural activities are performed by women. Also, livestock activity is capillary in the city, and not just on the city green belt. In fact, in the houses' courtyards, the majority of families raise small animals such as goats, sheep and especially poultry such as chicken, ducks and pigeons, and they grow fruit and vegetables.

The production of fish and seafood is also a potential source of food for Pemba; however, fishing activity, although it is highly diffused and practiced regularly, is done with rudimental techniques that do not provide much more than what is needed by the fishermen's families. Fishing is practiced both in the open sea and in aquaculture. Due to the strong tides that characterize the seafront, the activities performed by inhabitants are varied: during the low tide, women and children grab small fishes and sea fruits, while when the tide is high, fishermen go offshore to fish from their traditional boat (usually self-constructed) called *dhow*.

Commerce is also diffused in the city, although it is characterized by informality. According to the PEDM, the network of commerce is made up of over 800 formal commercial activities compared to the over 2200 informal ones. Every neighbourhood has its own informal market where everyday commerce is practiced. Other than these, there are the formal markets, which are mainly shops and supermarkets and five municipal markets (Batatas, Central, Mbaguia, Cariacó, Noviane).

Industry represents a small sector in Pemba. A diagnosis by the PEDM has revealed that Pemba does not produce one-sixth of the needs for goods and services consumed by its inhabitants, even if the city is potentially an expanding market for many products that can be locally produced.

Today the Pemba industrial sector specializes in the construction industry, mills, sawmills, carpentry, cashew processing, shrimp processing, poultry processing, purified water packaging, bakeries, crafts and pottery (Conselho Municipal da Cidade de Pemba, 2014).

Tourism is also relevant for the local economy, and the municipality envisions it will increase even if the conflicts started in 2019 in the Cabo Delgado region threaten its development. According to the municipal data, today the city has 23 hotels, rated from two to five stars, with approximately 2300 beds. Pemba was always known as a lively city, with a good nightlife, bars, music and cultural spaces, beautiful beaches and good airport connections to the main cities of Mozambique and to the Quirimbas National Park. However, today tourists, especially international tourists, are asking for better quality than the city can offer.

The transportation system is also a good source of employment. The main transportation systems present in Pemba are *semicollectivos* or *chapa* (informal transportation), public transports, taxis, cars, motorbikes and bicycles. Four public bus lines were dedicated to Pemba's public transportation, but they cover less than 20% of the urban demand for transportation. The answer to the remaining need of the city for public transportation is provided by the informal sector.

Infrastructures

The network of streets – Pemba's urban morphology is linked to the topography of the city. The slope on the bay side did not allow a homogeneous formal urbanization of the western side, and the city expanded on the eastern side, along and past Wimbi Beach in the Eduardo Mondlane administrative division.

The city has five main paved streets (*avenidas*): (1) the Avenida 25 de Setembro, which cuts through the city in a north-south direction and follows the highest contour line of the city; (2) the Avenida da Marginal, which, starting from the Cimento neighbourhood, follows the eastern coast; (3) three avenidas that cut transversally through the city and link the Avenida da Marginal with the Avenida 25 de Setembro, starting from the north; these are the Avenida 16 de Junho; (4) the Avenida Eduardo Mondlane and (5) the Avenida do Chai.

The city is currently developing along the Avenida 25 de Setembro with the neighbourhoods of Mahate and Muxara and along the eastern coast (with an unpaved prolongation of the Avenida da Marginal) with Chuiba.

Besides the main *avenidas*, a net of unpaved streets, called *ruas*, is present in all of the neighbourhoods. In addition to this, there is a network of unregistered streets and alleys.

According to the data of the PEDM, the street network of Pemba consists of 200 km, of which 70 km are classified and 130 km are non-classified. Among the 70 km of classified streets, 47 are asphalted, 11 are made of planed earth and 12 are constructed from natural earth. The Avenida 25 Setembro, the main street, is in good condition, but the rest of the asphalted streets contain holes, missing asphalt and have other problems. The 52% of non-asphalted streets are in good condition, even though several problems may arise during the rainy season.

The port – The port of Pemba is given in concession to the company *Portos de Cabo Delgado*, by the Central Government and collects the national and international fluxes of ships. The port has a limited capacity; however, it is used by the industries of wood, oil, natural gas and agriculture. The port has deep access, between 60 m and 70 m in its entrance, between 10 m and 40 m in its medium area, and up to 25 m for the anchorage at the quay. Furthermore, it is easy to access the port in any weather conditions and at any time of day. Ships with a draft of up to 6 m can enter; however, steering is necessary due to some isolated dangers, such as rocks and choral benches, which are present in the entrance canal and delimitated by the Said Ali point (north) and Romero point (south), both signalled by lighthouses.

The airport – Pemba's airport is the most important of the province, and it deals with domestic and regional traffic. It is located in the centre of the city, bordering the Alto Gingone neighbourhood, and it was rehabilitated in

2013. Its track is 3 km long. In the years 2011–2014, it transported 80,000 passengers (61,000 domestic travellers).

Water, electricity and telecommunications – According to the analysis of the PEDM, the capacity of the municipal system's water supply is 10,000 m³ per day, and the number of houses connected to the net in 2014 was 5,633, while there were 137 public wells. The system has a high overall level of water leakage (around 15%), and it is not satisfying the water needs of the local population, especially during the dry season. Furthermore, the PEDM analysis reports that the public electric network covers 56% of the houses, with a capacity of 110 MWH. The number of private connections is increasing, and in 2013, there were 8,129 customers. The project *Estratégias de Desenvolvimento do Corredor de Nacala 2015–2035* is going to improve the electricity supply in Pemba with the construction of a secondary electric line that will provide electricity to the companies working in the mega projects of oil and gas.

The telecommunications infrastructure is provided by the company *Telecommunicações de Moçambique* (TDM) and from the mobile network provided by mCel, Vodacom and Movitel. All the operators transmit voice, data and images with the optical fibre. The fixed telephones installed are 3,599 units, including television, Internet and data transmission. The city receives radio and television signals and has local newspapers.

The sanitation system – The sanitation system in Pemba mainly consists of scattered sceptic tanks in the neighbourhood of Cimento and of improved and traditional latrines in the other neighbourhoods. However, in 2013 in the suburban neighbourhoods, latrines consisted of less than the 70% of the sanitation system, and many of the inhabitants still practice open-air defecation.

Garbage collection covers less than 50% of the city; the accumulation of garbage is widespread, and sometimes it is privately interred in the courtyards.

Water drainage is lacking in most of the city areas, which generates great problems during the rainy season.

In the PEDM the municipality highlights the following seven problems: (1) degradation of several public streets; (2) soil erosion; (3) existence of non-classified streets; (4) lack of water supply; (5) low-quality energy supply; (6) limited port capacity and (7) lack of a drainage system and sanitation system.

Social system

Education – The population has a high percentage of illiteracy due to the low level of schooling, both in adults and youngsters. The management of the school system was previously made by the Ministry of Education, but it is now managed by the municipality. The first schools managed by the

Municipality of Pemba are those of Chuiba, Koba, Muxara A, Muxara B and Paquitequete.

Health care – The city has four "sanitary units" called *Centros de Saúde* in Paquitequete, Ingonane, Chuiba and Muxara; however, all of the neighbourhoods have a smaller local centre. The city also benefits from the province hospital, which offers more diversified services. One of the main health problems in Pemba is HIV/AIDS with 7% of the population infected. Cholera and malaria are two other important illnesses found in the city (Conselho Municipal da Cidade de Pemba, 2014).

Notes

1 www.istituto-oikos.org/progetti/emergenza-mozambico. Last visited April 2, 2020.
2 Direito de Uso e Aproveitamento da Terra (right of use and benefit of the land).

Reference list

Newitt, M. (2017). *A Short History of Mozambique*. London: C. Hurst & Co. Ltd.

Documents and reports

Conselho Municipal da Cidade de Pemba. (2014). *Plano Estrategico de Desenvolvimento 2014–2018*.
OCHA (United Nations Office for the Coordination of Humanitarian Affairs). (2019). *Mozambique: Cyclone Idai & Floods*. Situation Report No.22. www.unocha.org/southern-eastern-africa.
UN Habitat, USAID, Conselho Municipal da Cidade de Pemba. (2016). *Avaliação Rápida da Situação de Infra-estruturas habitacional na Cidade de Pemba no contexto de adaptação as mudanças climáticas Bairros de Paquitequete, Cariacó (Chibuabuari), Josina Machel, Chuiba e Eduardo Mondlane*.

Articles and briefings

Cambaza, E., Mongo, E., Anapakala, E., Nhambire, R., Singo, J., and Machava, E. (2019). Outbreak of Cholera Due to Cyclone Kenneth in Northern Mozambique. *International Journal of Environmental Research and Public Health*, Volume 16. https://doi.org/10.3390/ijerph16162925. www.mdpi.com/journal/ijerph.
COSACA (the Humanitarian Agencies Group Consisting of Oxfam, CARE and Save the Children). 2019. *Cosaca Joint Agency Briefing Note. From Cyclone to Food Crisis*. Oxford: Oxfam GB. https://doi.org/10.21201/2019.4634
Hope, M. (2019). Cyclones in Mozambique May Reveal Humanitarian Challenges of Responding to a New Climate Reality. *The Lancet Planetary Health*, Volume 3, pp. e338–e339.
Pozniak, A., Atzori, A., Marotta, C., Di Gennaro, F., and Putoto, G. (2020). HIV Continuity of Care After Cyclone Idai in Mozambique. *The Lancet HIV*, Volume 7, pp. e159–e160. www.thelancet.com/hiv

5 Unpacking four settlement types in Pemba

The four selected neighbourhoods: selection and survey

Four neighbourhoods were selected for the analysis: Alto Gingone, Paquite-quete, Chuiba and Natite. These have different morphological and architectural features as they represent the local culture of living in different periods of Pemba's expansion as clearly visible in Figure 5.1. The integrated analysis gives a representation and determines the prevailing typologies in these four neighbourhoods. The material produced within the survey and consequent analysis embraces five scales of detail: (1) the regional analysis at 1:5000, (2) the neighbourhoods analysis at 1:1000, (3) the blocks survey at 1:500, (4) the houses' survey of spaces and functions at 1:200 and (5) the objects within the houses represented and catalogued through photographs. This allowed for the determination of the prevailing houses' typologies in the four neighbourhoods and the detection of those most coherent with the traditional Swahili house type.

The neighbourhoods were identified during the preliminary documentation phase and then confirmed on site.

The parameters that allowed their selection were: (1) the age of the settlement; (2) the geographical conditions; (3) the demographical data; (4) accessibility to the main infrastructures and (5) the accessibility and safety of the neighbourhood.

Age of settlements – From the oldest to the youngest, it was possible to survey the settlements built in different times. Paquitequete was the first settlement to be built in Pemba; it belongs to the pre-colonial period. Then, Natite represents the indigenous residential neighbourhood of the period of the Portuguese colonial urban development, while Alto Gingone was born around the years of independence, and Chuiba is a rural settlement, which is now being included in the Pemba city as an ongoing stage of city expansion.

Geographical conditions – The four neighbourhoods have similar topographical conditions. When making the selection, the geographical homogeneity of the settlements was crucial to allow for the comparative analysis of the house typologies. All of them are settled on a plane area, and even though all of the neighbourhoods are closely related to the seafront, Paquitequete, Natite and Chuiba directly face the sea.

Demographical data – The neighbourhood selection process also took into account the number and the ethnicity of people living there. Concerning the number of inhabitants, only Chuiba differs, with between 4,000 and 9,000 people, while the other three neighbourhoods host between 9,000 and 22,000 people.

In spite of the homogeneity in the number of people, all of the areas differ significantly in terms of ethnic provenance. In fact, Mozambique hosts a plurality of ethnicities, and Pemba represents this mixture well. There are three main ethnic groups present in the four neighbourhoods: the Mwanì, an ethnic group of Arab provenance, mainly of Islamic religion. Historically, they were considered servants and submitted as such, but this ethnic group was always devoted to fishing and commercial activities. Paquitequete hosts a community of numerous Mwanì people; however, they also live in the other neighbourhoods in family cells.

Then there is the Macua ethnic group, which comes from an African tribe and whose people mainly adhere to Islamic and African beliefs. Groups of Macua can be found in Natite, Alto Gingone and Chuiba. This is a gentle population who shows respect for nature, and their society is traditionally patrilineal. A peculiarity is that both women and men wear a white beauty mask made from wood. Last but not least, there is the Maconde ethnic group, which also comes from an African tribe, but its people are known for their strength and for being the warriors who fought for the independence of Mozambique. The Macondes speak ChiMakonde (or Makonde) a language with Bantu origins. Traditionally, they follow animistic beliefs, but today many of them are Catholic or Muslim, and their society is matrilineal. Their people usually had their faces covered with tattoos, a tradition that has been abandoned by the latest generations, and they are famous for their artworks made from carved blackwood. Among the surveyed neighbourhoods in Pemba, they mainly live in Alto Gingone and Natite.

Accessibility to the main infrastructures – Each neighbourhood has the peculiarity of being connected to important infrastructures that serve and provide jobs to the whole settlement. Paquitequete stands close to the former Portuguese colonial settlement, Cimento, and the port. Natite was established for the indigenous workforce that worked in the Cimento neighbourhood, with its colonial families, commercial activities and infrastructures. Alto Gingone is separated from the airport only by a main street, while Chuiba, even though it lacks the main infrastructures and paved streets, faces the sea, where most of the people congregate for fishery activities.

Accessibility and safety of the neighbourhood – A further parameter used for the selection focussed on the feasibility of the survey in terms of neighbourhood accessibility and safety. The choice was made thanks to the community leaders who agreed to participate in the research and to put us in contact with the local inhabitants. According to the statistics, Pemba is a socially safe environment. The main threats documented by the PEDM are corruption, malaria and cholera. Generally, the population is open to dialogue with foreigners; however, the delicacy of the survey, asking people to enter their private space and to collect information about it, needed to be introduced and prepared by locals. The neighbourhood in which the most inhabitants refused to be part of the research was Natite, a very diversified community in terms of ethnic groups, and with a commercial area often frequented by foreigners and in which the sense of community is not perceivably as strong as in the other neighbourhoods. When inhabitants refused to collaborate, their plots were not surveyed; in drawings they are reported as "not surveyable".

Basic instruments for the survey – The on-site survey is a delicate moment. It is important to collect as much information as possible to reduce the number of inspections, but at the same time, it requires discretion and the tools used must be simple and cheap to allow easy dialogue with the inhabitants without being in the public eye. Therefore, the instruments to record the information were simple:

1   a compact photo camera, with the possibility of recording HD videos and with integrated GPS;
2   a mobile phone application to track paths via GPS;
3   a sketchbook to draw sketches using a simple pencil and eraser, useful also to take notes on the inhabitants' answers and to show them a graphic representation of the ongoing work;
4   tape measure;
5   laser distance metre;
6   Portuguese dictionary;
7   maps at 1:5000 and 1:1000 scales previously redrawn and printed.

Furthermore, all of the inhabitants were asked to provide the same basic information, such as the period in which the house was built, who the builder was, what the prevailing structure and construction technique were, the number of people living in the house, the composition of the family nucleus, the adults' occupations and the ethnic group.

Representation and interpretation – The representation and interpretation phase consisted of two preliminary steps. The first was implemented immediately after the on-site survey as it is very important to quickly redraw (first in sketches and then in digital) the acquired information to understand errors and review for missing data to plan the following inspections. The second step consisted of reordering, redrawing and systematizing the acquired data.

Local contacts – For the development of the on-site survey operations, the local contacts were fundamental. The survey was conduced by the author with

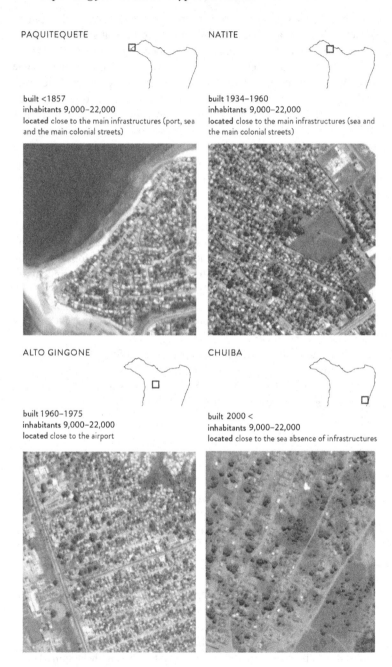

PAQUITEQUETE

built <1857
inhabitants 9,000–22,000
located close to the main infrastructures (port, sea
and the main colonial streets)

NATITE

built 1934–1960
inhabitants 9,000–22,000
located close to the main infrastructures (sea and
the main colonial streets)

ALTO GINGONE

built 1960–1975
inhabitants 9,000–22,000
located close to the airport

CHUIBA

built 2000 <
inhabitants 9,000–22,000
located close to the sea absence of infrastructures

Figure 5.1 Overview of the four neighbourhoods (by the author)
Source: Satellite images by Google Maps.

the help of a local tour guide from the *Associação de Guia de Tuchambane*, João Felisberto. He was the person who provided the connection to community leaders, accompanied us in the selected neighbourhoods' houses and translated, when needed, from the Swahili, Macua, Mwanì and Maconde languages to Portuguese. However, the involvement of all possible actors is crucial to the on-site operations and the comprehension of the context. Among the main associations and institutions that made the on-site survey possible were:

1   Agricultural department of the Municipality of Pemba – At this department it was possible to find 20th-century maps in a scale of 1:2000 and 1:5000 describing the plot dimensions and the street section.
2   Architetti Senza Frontiere – This contact was made in Milan, through Camillo Magni and Filippo Mascaretti. It was possible to visit their Ibo Island Project, called PHARO, in cooperation with Oikos.
3   ArqPAC – The historical archive of Pemba provided oral information on the area and the historical images.
4   Associação de guia de Turismo Tuchangane – The connection with this association was very important for the language and cultural intermediation.
5   GVC (Gruppi di Volontariato Civile) – This organization was contacted through Oikos NGO, and it created the contact with the Associação de Guia de Turismo.
6   Municipality of Pemba – Here it was possible to meet the staff of the municipality that presented the regulatory plans and the municipal vision.
7   Oikos NGO – The association is based in Milan and has also an office with guesthouse in Pemba and Ibo Island. The contact was made through Alessandro Floris, that previously worked on Pemba with Marcello De Carli, of the Politecnico di Milano. Oikos develops several projects in Cabo Delgado region.
8   UN Habitat Mozambique and USAID – The contact with UN Habitat, especially during their participatory meetings with the local community, enriched the research with information on the constructive techniques and elements of the houses in Pemba.
9   UNILURIO University of Pemba – The Director created the connection with an ongoing project by UN Habitat Mozambique, the Municipality of Pemba and USAID.

Formation and recent evolution

The city was born from a small nucleus and grew neighbourhood by neighbourhood as if each is a part of the urban fabric that reflects different stages of the city's development. Paquitequete was the first settlement in the city; it originated during the Swahili occupation and was used as a natural port. Then, in the 1930s, the port of Pemba was built close to the colonial areas of settlement (Baixa and Cimento). It followed the creation of the neighbourhoods Ingonane, Natite and Cariacò, which were then built with a regular grid of streets and plots. This regularity was interrupted by the informal growth that started at the end of the 1990s in Paquitequete and Cariacò (Pereira, 2012). Around the years of independence, with the construction of the airport, the Alto Gingone neighbourhood developed, and then the city expanded with the Eduardo Mondlane neighbourhood, along Wimbi Beach, where tourist attractions are located and services like beaches, resorts and hotels are offered. The same growth destiny is envisaged for the Chuiba neighbourhood, while Mahate and Muchara are supposed to develop as industrial and residential areas.

Looking at the selected neighbourhoods' evolution, through the layering of historical Google Earth images, it was possible to understand some elements of the typo-morphological development of the city. For example, in 2003, the surveyed block in the Paquitequete neighbourhood was already complete, and the main buildings and plot boundaries were already present. In the following years, only minor constructions were built, especially since 2010. Therefore, Paquitequete is a neighbourhood which, in its typo-morphological features, is stable, and the construction of additional buildings is probably due to the process of urbanization that the city is experiencing, with the consequent arrival of a greater number of inhabitants from the rural areas of the country. However, this has not highly impacted the neighbourhood.

On the contrary, in recent years, the urbanization process highly affected the Natite neighbourhood. In 2003, the surveyed block was mainly composed of the main constructions; latrines and plot boundaries were not always present, and in the cases in which the boundary was present, the main building retained a direct connection between the public space of the street and the private space of the house. Up to 2013, it is visibly an ongoing modification process but with minor additions to the built-up houses and to plot delimitations. However, between 2013 and 2016, the majority of the new buildings were constructed, all within the plots and with strong physical delimitations dividing the public and the private space, as though the increase in population made the inhabitants feel the need to increase their privacy and protect themselves by building up walls around their plot, strongly changing the relationship between the public and the private space.

Alto Gingone differs from the previous two; in fact, since 2003, the surveyed block in the Alto Gingone neighbourhood has not been affected by relevant changes. The typology, visible in the satellite images of 2003, followed the rules of the Swahili house typology, and they are still maintained. In time, several minor additions were made, but among these, few are the cases in which the original relationship between public and private space was not kept.

At the present stage, Chuiba also still keeps the original characteristics of living, even though, from 2007 to 2016, the houses of the surveyed block doubled, from five houses in 2007 to ten in 2016, and the settlement is supposed to increase even more because of the municipal city vision. In spite of this, the neighbourhood still enjoys a very free relationship between public and private space, reflecting the rural living habits. Plot boundaries are, in most cases, not present, even though the difference from the street to the house courtyard is perceivable, most noticeably by a different level of care of the sand floor, which dissuades passers-by from coming onto private property.

Urban morphology

Pemba's urban fabric types

According to Pereira, different types of urban fabrics characterize the urban morphology of Pemba: (1) the indigenous, (2) the colonial, (3) the popular urbanization of the 20th–21st century and (4) the informal settlement (Pereira, 2012).

The indigenous mainly corresponds to the Paquitequete neighbourhood, the first settlement of the city, located on the horn of the peninsula. Aside from the presence of one vehicle-accessible street, its alleys are temporary and narrow (sometimes less than 1 m wide). Houses are generally aligned along the street front, and they are usually in *pau à pique* one-storey high.

The colonial fabric is located in the areas of Baixa and Cimento, where concrete buildings are one or more storeys high. In this type of fabric, streets (mainly paved) have a regular course, and buildings align to the street front.

The popular urbanization of the 20th–21st-century urban fabric is present in all of the other neighbourhoods of the city. It consists of regular plots with variable dimensions based on when the plans were made. Constructions are mainly in *pau à pique*, and plots follow a Roman grid of distribution and are connected to the main street to which they are aligned. This type of fabric can be found in the selected neighbourhoods of Natite, Alto Gingone and Chuiba, even if the three neighbourhoods represent three different stages of the city's evolution.

The informal settlement fabric is characterized by irregularity in infrastructures, plot dimensions, houses' construction types and land ownership. These settlements are mainly concentrated in the area bordering the waste dump along the western coastline comprised by the port and the airport.

Selected neighbourhoods' plots and houses

To study the selected neighbourhoods' urban morphology, a 1:1000 scale was used on which elements were analyzed by layers and through historical aero-photogrammetric images, recorded by the Google Earth satellites since 2003, or 2007, focussing on the surveyed blocks.

The layers used are the voids and the built-up houses, the paved and unpaved streets, the broad-crowned vegetation, the public, semi-public and private space, the community functions and the built-up density, with the number of floors per building. This analysis shows the morphological differences of the four neighbourhoods, even though they all have in common the density of broad-crowned vegetation (see Figure 5.2), widely used in public and private spaces, and the number of floors, which is homogeneously one floor, with just a few exceptions in Alto Gingone and Natite.

Paquitequete originated based on the topography, with a resulting network of streets that follow the contour lines, and the plots and houses' distribution is organic. The courtyards are smaller, and the private space is mainly related to the built-up houses. On the contrary, Natite is made of a network of streets, and the plots and houses follow a regular matrix. The private space includes the open space of the courtyards. The public space is mainly related to the streets, and the main public space is where most of the community functions are performed. Natite is also hosting the headquarters of many international organizations. Also, Alto Gingone follows a matrix of streets in which plots are regularly designed. Courtyards are wider than those in Natite, but the concept of private and public space is also limited to the streets and the main communitarian spaces. However, the public and private space is mediated by the architectural element of the veranda which, standing on the street front, creates a direct connection between the house and the street. Chuiba differs from the other three neighbourhoods as it represents a peri-urban area which still has very strong rural characteristics. This neighbourhood is provided with a school, a mosque and a neighbourhood headquarters, but it lacks most of the public services, including a network of streets, as it is reached only by the unpaved extension of the Avenida da Marginal. However, the houses are aligned to the main unpaved paths, and plots are not fenced.

Here boundaries are almost absent, but houses are still aligned and follow the disposition of a matrix. In this situation, public and private spaces compenetrate, even though it is well understandable that there is a limit between the public and the private and the behaviour changes related to it.

As previously mentioned, with the urbanization process, the number of constructions within the plot tends to increase and with it the need to increase the privacy level. As a consequence, the plot boundaries are built and gradually become thicker, and the number of inhabitants in the neighbourhood increases and the distance between the houses shortens as well.

Figure 5.2 Neighbourhood analysis: broad-crowned vegetation
Source: Corinna Del Bianco

Public, semi-public and private spaces

Public space is present and well respected by the inhabitants, and usually it is located in specific areas of the neighbourhood where most of the public functions are located. In each selected neighbourhood, this centre is present. Among the more relevant functions it hosts are the neighbourhood headquarters, the school, the health care centre, the commercial activities and, in the cases of Chuiba and Paquitequete, the mosque. In Paquitequete, the soccer field is central to community life, and it is used during the day for different activities. Around this, the public functions are organized, and sometimes even the political representation of the FRELIMO party (such as in Natite and Alto Gingone) is also present. Paquitequete, Natite and Chuiba are also characterized by the beach, a public space used for accessing the sea, for fishing, for seafood collection and also for leisure time. However, open-air defecation and garbage dissemination in the beach areas are affecting the hygienic conditions.

Public space is strongly perceived in all the neighbourhoods: in each area a main square is present where the community activities are performed. As it is clearly shown in Figure 5.3, in the neighbourhoods where plots are fenced and clearly designed, such as Natite and Alto Gingone, but also in Paquitequete, the distinction between public and private space is clear, and no semi-public space is present. On the contrary, in Chuiba, where plots are present but not fenced, the courtyards become a semi-public space, where people can pass, even if the owners perform part of the family's private activities there and keep them clean and tidy.

Streets

The street network reflects the planning time and the accessibility of the neighbourhoods. As shown in Figure 5.4, Paquitequete has one unpaved driveway, following the contour line, from which a network of spontaneous alleys and pathways branches off. There is no real regulation for the alleys; therefore, it can happen that someone builds his/her own house where a passage is located. Natite's street network branches off the paved coastal Avenida da Marginal; it is unpaved but is regular and vehicle accessible. Here, blocks can host up to 20 (or more) plots in width and two in depth. Alto Gingone streets were designed with a very rigid matrix. Blocks have minor variations in size because they tend to be very regular as this settlement is the result of the 1980's Villagization Policy. Chuiba is served by the unpaved extension of the Avenida da Marginal. On the east side of the avenida, pathways branch off to the beach, while on the west side, unpaved but regular lanes and alleys serve the houses and services of the neighbourhood. Plots, even though in most cases these are not physically defined, are aligned to the passages.

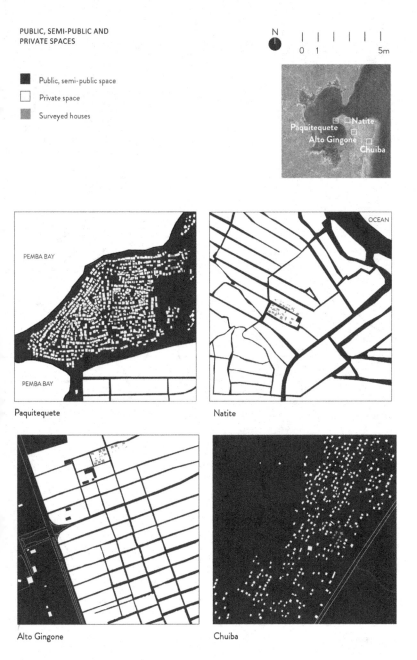

Figure 5.3 Neighbourhood analysis: public, semi-public and private spaces
Source: Corinna Del Bianco

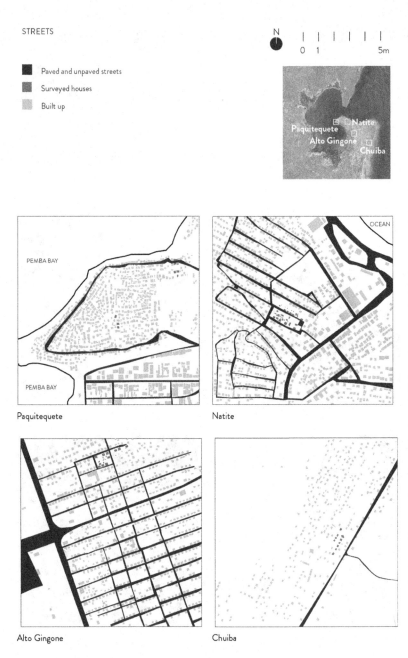

Figure 5.4 Neighbourhood analysis: streets
Source: Corinna Del Bianco

Built up

The analysis of the built-up houses in the four neighbourhoods, summerized in the maps of Figure 5.5, revealed that in all of them, despite the infrastructural differences, there is a regular alignment to the street front. Natite, Alto Gingone and Chuiba follow a regular rectangular plot structure, while Paquitequete follows the area's topographic characteristics. Furthermore, constructions are also regular in size and in density, except for Paquitequete, where plots have neither dimensions nor regular forms.

Floor numbers

The houses' prevailing typology and construction techniques cause the low density of the built-up houses (Figure 5.6). The resulting landscape is dominated by one-story houses. The exceptions are primarily the result of colonial buildings in Baixa, recent foreign investment in Natite and buildings related to the operation of the airport in Alto Gingone.

Community functions

Thanks to the country's socialist welfare, each neighbourhood has its own facilities, such as the neighbourhood headquarters, the health centre and the school. The buildings hosting these functions are located in central areas of the neighbourhood, where the main religious and commercial activities can also be found. Commerce is widely spread in Natite, and it is not present at all in Chuiba. In the neighbourhoods facing the sea, the beach is an important communitarian space; in fact, most of the men go fishing, especially in Chuiba and Paquitequete, where accessing the sea is easier than in Natite. When not in the sea, boats, usually *dhows*, are left on the beach, and men gather around them. The beach is also used by women and kids who collect seafood when tides are low. Beaches are also used for defecation and to throw away trash; this habit makes these areas unhygienic and subject to the proliferation of bacteria. Peculiarities can be found in each neighbourhood, such as the airport in Alto Gingone, where people work and gather, the public radio antenna in Natite, and the well-known soccer field of Paquitequete. This layer is reported in the maps of Figure 5.7.

Houses' spaces and functions

During the on-site survey, over 50 houses were surveyed, and among them 46 are reported as they could provide the same level of detail. Among the 46 surveyed houses, 6 are in Paquitequete, 24 in Natite, 10 in Alto Gingone and 6 in Chuiba.

Figure 5.5 Neighbourhood analysis: built up
Source: Corinna Del Bianco

Figure 5.6 Neighbourhood analysis: floor numbers
Source: Corinna Del Bianco

Figure 5.7 Neighbourhood analysis: community functions
Source: Corinna Del Bianco

Two architectural elements were present in all of the houses of the four neighbourhoods: the veranda and the courtyard. As visible in Figures 5.8 and 5.9, the veranda stands on two sides of the main building and is the link between open and closed spaces, and in some cases also between public and private spaces. The house is conceived as a sequence of open and covered spaces within the plot. The plot dimensions are irregular in Paquitequete and Cariacò but are generally regular in the other neighbourhoods, and they vary from 15 m x 15 m up to 20 m x 30 m.

In most of the neighbourhoods, the plot is delimited by a physical boundary that increases in thickness and material durability as the density of the area increases. The prevailing materials used for the boundaries are bamboo sticks, interlaced or simply aligned, and fixed together with wooden bars with nails, and cement blocks.

The focus on the houses in the selected neighbourhoods was developed with the on-site architectural survey at the 1:500 and the 1:200 scales and photo reportage. At the 1:500, the surveyed blocks both in plan and section are represented in order to focus on the relationships between the public and private spaces and the open and closed spaces. The Paquitequete neighbourhood offers a variety of relationships which did not allow the determination of a detailed prevailing typology, while this was possible in the Natite neighbourhood, where, being very dense, street fronts are not permeable and are built with thick boundaries. Furthermore, usually the constructions there are built within the perimeter of the plot. What concerns the Alto Gingone houses is that the relationship between public and private space is well connected by the element of the veranda, present in the majority of houses, both on the street and in the courtyard. There, plots are fenced, and the main house construction stands on the plot perimeter. On the contrary, Chuiba's houses are not characterized by fences, and the relationship between the private and public space is completely free. These typological and morphological differences create different community relationships in the four neighbourhoods.

The survey of spaces and functions within the houses is reported with the house sheets including the plan schemes at the scale of 1:200 with a description of the date, builder, number of inhabitants, construction technique and ethnic group of the dwellers. A selection of one of the most significant survey sheets per neighbourhood is reported in Figures 5.10 for Paquitequete, 5.11 for Natite, 5.12 for Alto Gingone and 5.13 for Chuiba. Each house was surveyed thanks to its inhabitant, who opened the house doors, and in most cases allowed photos to be taken of him/herself and of the private space of the house, and was interviewed. The interaction with the locals was crucial for this work, and their portraits complete the house sheets. Besides the inhabitant's portrait, each sheet consists of the drawing of the house plan completed by the photography of the street front of the houses and by the sketches made during the survey. For the purpose of this publication one house sheet per each neighbourhood was selected along with an extract of the photo reportage.

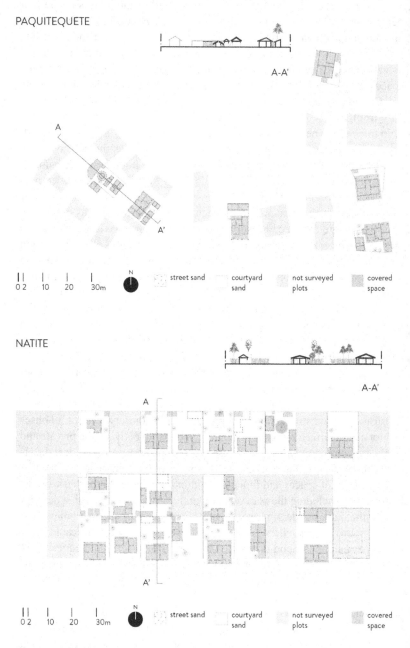

Figure 5.8 Paquitequete and Natite surveyed block plans and sections
Source: Corinna Del Bianco

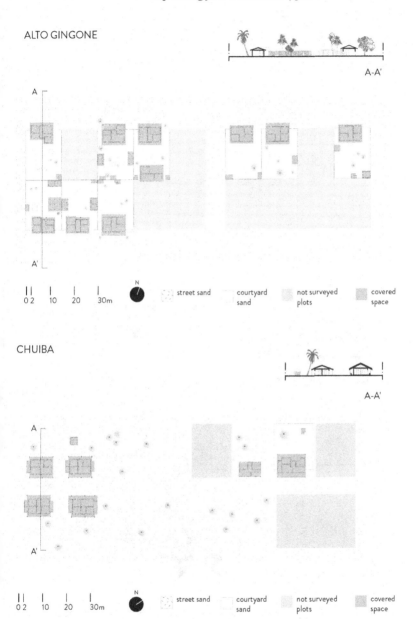

Figure 5.9 Alto Gingone and Chuiba surveyed block plans and sections

Source: Corinna Del Bianco

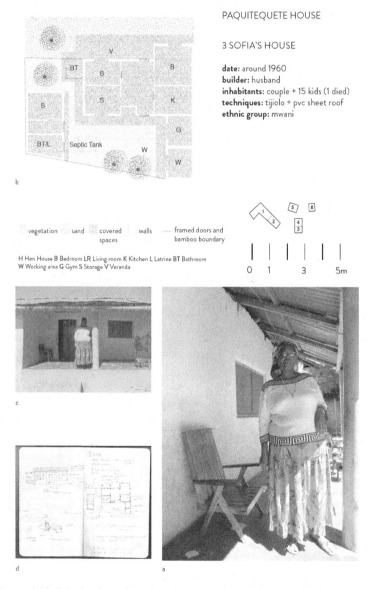

PAQUITEQUETE HOUSE

3 SOFIA'S HOUSE

date: around 1960
builder: husband
inhabitants: couple + 15 kids (1 died)
techniques: tijiolo + pvc sheet roof
ethnic group: mwani

vegetation   sand   covered   walls   —— framed doors and
spaces   bamboo boundary

H Hen House B Bedroom LR Living room K Kitchen L Latrine BT Bathroom
W Working area G Gym S Storage V Veranda

0   1   3   5m

Figure 5.10 Sample of Paquitequete's survey sheet. (a) Sofia is one of the community leaders of Paquitequete. She is aware of the infrastructural difficulties of the neighbourhood, and she is very proud of her house. She and her second husband live in the house and have additional rooms for guests. They are planning to build a bathroom inside the house. They do not have a latrine but a proper WC connected to a septic tank. (b) Sofia's house plan. (c) Entrance from the street side to one of the buildings of the house. Sofia is standing in the veranda. (d) Survey sketches and notes

Source: Corinna Del Bianco and Sofia

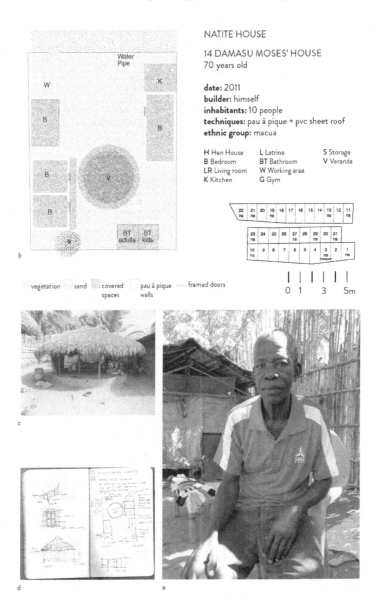

NATITE HOUSE

14 DAMASU MOSES' HOUSE
70 years old

date: 2011
builder: himself
inhabitants: 10 people
techniques: pau à pique + pvc sheet roof
ethnic group: macua

H Hen House	L Latrine	S Storage
B Bedroom	BT Bathroom	V Veranda
LR Living room	W Working area	
K Kitchen	G Gym	

vegetation sand covered spaces pau à pique walls framed doors

Figure 5.11 Sample of Natite's survey sheet. (a) Damasu Moses was a pharmacist. He is 70 years old, and now he has retired. He is very proud of his family and of his grandchildren. He built a circular veranda for them and also two latrines, one for the boys and one for the girls. (b) Damasu Moses' house plan. (c) View of the circular veranda. (d) Survey sketches and notes

Source: Corinna Del Bianco and Damasu Moses

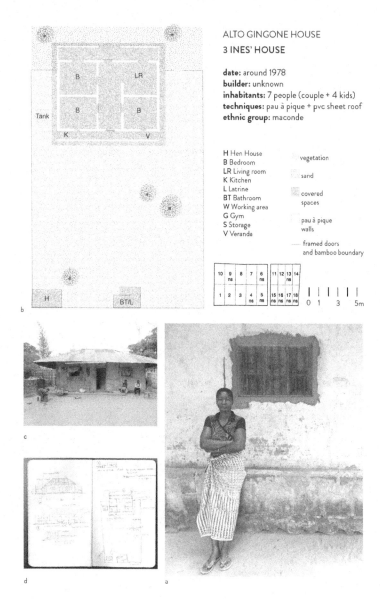

ALTO GINGONE HOUSE

3 INES' HOUSE

date: around 1978
builder: unknown
inhabitants: 7 people (couple + 4 kids)
techniques: pau à pique + pvc sheet roof
ethnic group: maconde

H Hen House
B Bedroom
LR Living room
K Kitchen
L Latrine
BT Bathroom
W Working area
G Gym
S Storage
V Veranda

vegetation

sand

covered spaces

pau à pique walls

framed doors and bamboo boundary

Figure 5.12 Sample of Alto Gingone's survey sheet. (a) Ines is one of the community leaders of Alto Gingone. She lives in this house since around 1978. (b) Ines' house plan. (c) Entrance from the courtyard to one of the buildings of the house. (d) Survey sketches and notes

Source: Corinna Del Bianco and Ines

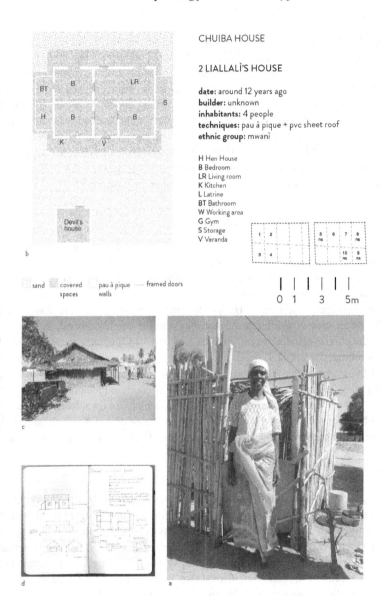

CHUIBA HOUSE

2 LIALLALÌ'S HOUSE

date: around 12 years ago
builder: unknown
inhabitants: 4 people
techniques: pau à pique + pvc sheet roof
ethnic group: mwani

H Hen House
B Bedroom
LR Living room
K Kitchen
L Latrine
BT Bathroom
W Working area
G Gym
S Storage
V Veranda

sand / covered spaces / pau à pique walls / framed doors

0 1 3 5m

Figure 5.13 Sample of Chuiba's survey sheet. (a) In the portrait, Liallalì is standing in front of her "house of Devil." This is a sacred space, and she uses it to pray the devil to stay away from her and from her family. (b) Liallali's house plan. (c) View of the house side from the street. (d) Survey sketches and notes

Source: Corinna Del Bianco and Liallalì

Structure

There are at least two constructions within the courtyards: the main building and the hygienic services, such as a bathroom and latrine. The main building is usually made of a wooden structure, often simply leaning on the sand or in other cases on a concrete slab about 10 cm thick. Walls, internal and external, are usually made in *pau à pique*: two layers of bamboo sticks filled with stones and mud. Among those surveyed, only a few examples were in concrete blocks or in bamboo sticks tied together with wooden bars. Vertical finishing is often absent, and, if it is present, it is in *matope* (Swahili word for mud) which can be of different colours, from light brown to red. The roof is made of a wooden structure and covered in vegetal materials or in metal sheets.

Relationship with the boundary

The main construction is located in relation to the boundary. In Natite, the denser area, it stands within the boundary; in Alto Gingone it stands in between the boundary; and in Chuiba, where boundaries are not physical, it stands aligned to the street side. In Paquitequete, it is usually aligned to the street side but with many exceptions. The position of the construction in relation to the boundary creates a different relationship with the neighbourhood, as reported in the photographic survey of Figures 5.14 and 5.15. In Natite, where the need for intimacy is stronger, streets are delimited by blind walls, and the perception of the intimacy is much more urban. In Alto Gingone, the verandas that are standing on the street side create a strong neighbourhood relationship, merging the interior with the exterior. In Chuiba, where plots are completely permeable as they are not fenced, the relationship of the house and of its inhabitants with the neighbourhood is much stronger and characterized by stronger connections.

Functions and their distribution

Regarding the functions and their distribution within the house, the main building is used for sleeping, resting and for storage. One surveyed case in Paquitequete also hosts a commercial activity, selling food and household products. The interiors of the building are usually distributed by a central corridor that links one entrance to the symmetrical one, and it distributes four rooms of similar dimensions, two on one side and two on the other. One of these rooms, usually the one facing the street side, is used as a living room; the others are used as bedrooms.

Elements and objects

The elements of the public and the private spaces are documented through a photographic analysis per neighbourhood, taking into account the main and secondary streets (Figure 5.14), the street fronts (Figure 5.15), the covered spaces in their interiors, roofs and verandas, the courtyards, the openings, in particular doors and windows (Figure 5.16), the elements of personal hygiene, such as the bathroom and the latrines, and the objects. As the objects within the houses were very few and poor, they were classified according to their use, related to fire, water (for its supply, collection and use), food and living.

A focus on the materials and textures (Figure 5.17) used for the vertical and horizontal finishing and structure is present, and the exceptions to the rule are also documented.

At the neighbourhood level, the community functions are represented here for the neighbourhood headquarters, commercial activities, schools, religious spaces, services and international contributions.

The elements are first described and then summarized in Table 5.1 comparing the four neighbourhoods and the Swahili traditional typology in order to find the characteristics of variance and permanence from this typology.

Paving

The type of paving inside the house embraces a wide range of varieties, from concrete with decorations, to concrete without decorations, to plastic coverings, to clean sand. Clean sand characterizes the flooring of all the surveyed courtyards, and this is distinguished from the street paving, which is usually in dirty sand. This distinction occurs also in those houses that do not have a physical plot boundary and defines the limit between what is public and what is private space.

Openings

The openings have the function of letting air circulate, but often they are obscured for privacy and security reasons. As a consequence, the interiors are usually dark and not properly ventilated. Types vary a lot in the different neighbourhoods (see Figure 5.16), and Chuiba has the largest variety of opening types. Windows can be voids within the wooden structure without obscuration or obscured by metal sheets or fabrics. Window frames, when they are present, can be made with industrial materials or alternatively in an artisanal manner. The industrial window frames can be made of wood or iron, or with iron gratings and/or glass. The artisanal window frames are always framed in wood and can be decorated and have a mosquito net. Doors are framed and delimited within the structure and are made of wood, industrial or handmade, or of iron.

Usually the openings are symmetrical both on the street side and in the courtyard, with the exception of Paquitequete, where a variety of solutions were found.

Figure 5.14 Photographic survey of the main and secondary streets per neighbourhood

Source: Corinna Del Bianco

STREET FRONTS   COURTYARDS

Figure 5.15 Photographic survey of the street fronts and the courtyards per neighbourhood

Source: Corinna Del Bianco

WINDOWS

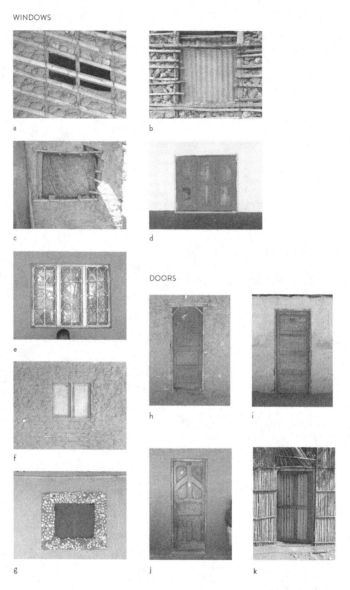

DOORS

Figure 5.16 Photographic survey of the openings: examples of windows and doors. (a) Window created within the structure. (b) Window with metal obscuring. (c) Window with tissues obscuring. (d) Fixed industrial window. (e) Iron grating and glasses. (f) Fixed wooden window. (g) Decorated window with mosquito net. (h) Door with wooden closure. (i) Handmade wooden closure. (j) Industrial wooden closure. (k) Iron sheet on wooden frame

Source: Corinna Del Bianco

TEXTURES

VERTICAL

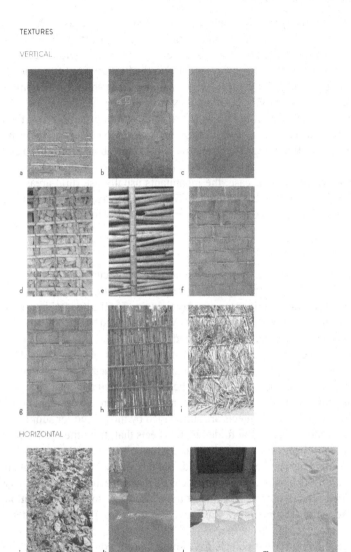

HORIZONTAL

Figure 5.17 Photographic survey of the prevailing textures: vertical and horizontal. (a) Vertical walls finishing: matope. (b) Vertical walls finishing: matope. (c) Vertical walls finishing: red matope. (d) Vertical structural element: pau à pique. (e) Vertical structural element: bamboo. (f) Vertical structural element: concrete blocks. (g) Vertical boundaries: concrete blocks. (h) Vertical boundaries: canes. (i) Vertical boundaries: straws. (j) Horizontal material: dirty sand. (k) Horizontal material: concrete without decorations. (l) Horizontal material: concrete with decorations. (m) Horizontal material: clean sand

Source: Corinna Del Bianco

Bathrooms and latrines

The other always-present construction within the yard hosts the hygienic functions of the bathroom and latrine. This construction is made to be moved within the yard as there is no sewage system; therefore, it is considered as temporary but is always located in the furthest point from the house, on the back side of the yard. Its surrounding walls are made of bamboo or plastic materials or fabric. Often, they have no over-head covering.

The latrine is often built beside the bathroom in order to reuse the bath water to wash away the dirt. It often consists of two holes: one for urinating and one for defecating. The urination hole can be about 50 cm deep and the defecation hole around 80 cm deep. In some houses of Chuiba, the latrine is not present; in that case, the inhabitants usually use rural areas and the beach for defecating and urinating. Waste of every type is usually buried or left at the edges of the neighbourhoods or buried in the courtyards.

Objects

Within the houses, a number of objects were documented and classified according to their use. Objects are very rudimental and poor but constitute elements of the inhabitants' everyday living and of the houses' interiors. For the purpose of this research objects were classified according to their use wether related to fire, water, food and everyday life.

Fire-related objects are used mainly for cooking as there is no need for heating. The portable ovens can be made of iron or terracotta, and charcoal slack is employed for cooking. They can be moved around the open spaces of the courtyard or of the veranda but sometimes are used inside the main building.

The water-related objects are subdivided by those used for supplies, such as the water pipe and the folded metal sheets that, from the roofs, reach the tanks to collect rain water, those used for collection and storage, such as tanks off the ground or underground, and those used for water use and transportation, such as buckets and dispensers that are usually made of plastic.

Food-related objects are mainly those used for storage, preparation and conservation of alimentary stuff, and they span from the simplest tissue or basket to electric refrigerators.

Also, living-related objects have some kind of contrast, from technological ones to the most simple and rudimental. For example, as in many African countries, kids of Pemba play soccer with balls made of plastic bags. Within the neighbourhoods' centre can be found something that in Western countries we are no longer used to seeing: an office typewriter. However, in houses, often there is a TV (and therefore an antenna in the yard) or even a computer or a refrigerator, but most of the adults use a mobile phone. Aside from these particular objects, life consists of very simple and basic elements. Most of the activities are done while sitting on the floor in the courtyard; usually a few benches are available in the house but not enough for all of the inhabitants. The same holds true for beds and tables. But this also depends on the family who lives in and owns the house. In any case, the most common object is the *capulana*, a stole of fabric about 1 x 2 m that is used for multiple purposes, from a skirt, to a purse, to a baby/child carrier, to a curtain, tablecloth and so on.

Types analysis and typology determination

Through the schematization of the surveyed houses in covered and open areas (Figure 5.18), it was possible to superpose the surveyed plans per neighbourhood. From this superposition the prevailing typology per neighbourhood is detected (Figure 5.19). Each typology is then analyzed for its relationships with public space and reinserted in an inter-scalar analysis to better understand the strength and weaknesses of each house type. As described in the conclusions, the most interesting typology to be used in the city expansion is the one of Alto Gingone, characterized by a wide courtyard, used for poultry and kitchen gardens, and two verandas that create a strong relationship with the public space.

The Mozambican house originated mainly from two already-present typologies: the circular house and the Swahili house. The circular one was mainly used in rural areas in the north of Mozambique and was made by a boundary in which huts for family members were gathered around a central tree. The Swahili house was more adaptable to urban contexts as, having a rectangular plan, it was easily aggregated. The resulting combination was the Mozambican Swahili house, made of a sequence of covered and uncovered spaces within a plot. During the colonial period, mainly materials and dimensional changes were made to the typology, and today the result is the one visible in the Alto Gingone neighbourhood.

All of the surveyed house plans were schematized in covered and uncovered areas in order to get the average dimensional ranges and the quantity of built and unbuilt spaces within the plots. The schemes where then superposed to determine the prevailing typology per each neighbourhood. From this superposition it was possible to establish the characteristics of each neighbourhood house in its dimensional and functional elements. From the superposition of the plans of the surveyed houses per neighbourhood it was also possible to determine the main typology per neighbourhood.

From this analysis it can be concluded that the inhabitants, who are usually also the builders, organize the space in a very similar way, both for the internal distribution of the building and of the plot. Furthermore, they perceive similarly also the relationship to the public space of the street. In addition to that, the materials used do not vary much even if they, like the opening frames, constitute symbols of class recognition. The typology found in the neighbourhood of Alto Gingone is the one that corresponds the most to the traditional Swahili typology.

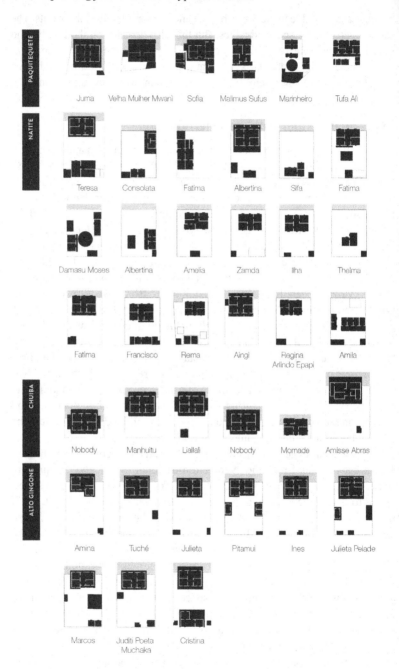

Figure 5.18 Schematic plans of the surveyed houses. In black the covered spaces, in white the uncovered spaces and in grey the street

Source: Corinna Del Bianco

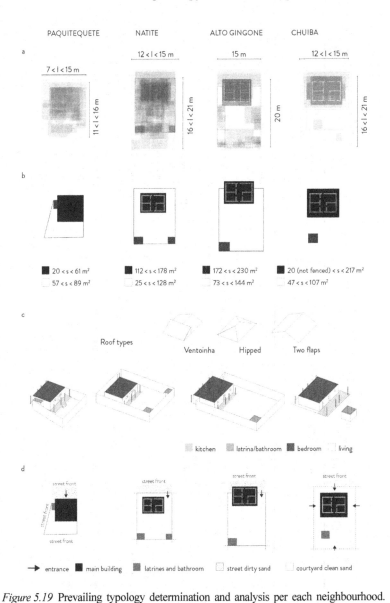

Figure 5.19 Prevailing typology determination and analysis per each neighbourhood.
(a) Plans superposition. (b) Prevailing typology main scheme.
(c) Axonometrical view of the prevailing typology per neighbourhood.
(d) Relationship of the prevailing house typology with the open public/not covered private and covered spaces

Source: Corinna Del Bianco

Table 5.1 Table comparing the main characteristics and elements of the Mozambican house, from its traditional Swahili typology to the ones of the four selected neighbourhoods

		Traditional Swahili typology (north of Mozambique)	Paquitequete 2016	Natite 2016	Alto Gingone 2016	Chuiba 2016
Street		present, unpaved	present, unpaved	present, unpaved, paved	present, unpaved, paved	present, unpaved
Boundaries (street fronts)		present (in urban context) absent (in rural context)	present (vegetal and mineral)	present (vegetal and mineral)	present (vegetal and mineral)	partially present (vegetal)
Covered spaces	**Walls**	pau à pique	pau à pique (a few in concrete blocks)	pau à pique	pau à pique (a few in concrete blocks)	pau à pique
	Roof	vegetal	vegetal/pvc /zinc	pvc/zinc	vegetal/pvc /zinc	vegetal/zinc
	Veranda	present	present	partially present	partially present	present
Courtyards		living/working/cooking	living/working/cooking	living/working/cooking	living/working/cooking	living/working/cooking
Openings	**doors**	not framed	industrial/artisanal	industrial/artisanal	industrial/artisanal	industrial/artisanal
	windows	not framed	industrial/artisanal	industrial/artisanal	industrial/artisanal	industrial/artisanal
Personal hygiene		outside the plot	latrine and bathroom	latrine and bathroom	latrine and bathroom	outside the plot and latrine and bathroom

Objects					
Fire related	charcoal	charcoal	charcoal	charcoal	charcoal
Water related	vegetal	plastic	plastic	plastic	plastic
Food related	vegetal	plastic	plastic	plastic	plastic
Living activities related	artisanal	industrial	industrial	industrial	industrial
Textures					
Vertical	matope	matope	matope	matope	matope
Horizontal	sand	Sand/concrete/plastic	Sand/concrete/plastic	Sand/concrete/plastic	Sand/concrete/plastic
Exceptions to the rule	–	bidet	Concrete bricks	Flowerbed/decorations	House of devil/decorations
Community functions	Local	Institutional/international	Institutional/international	Institutional/international	Institutional
Inhabitants	–	Mainly Mwani	Mainly Macua	Mainly Maconde	Mainly Mwani

New characters of living

The urban lifestyle, the number of urban inhabitants and globalization, influence the house typology, and in the four neighbourhoods, this process is homogeneously distributed. In all of the survey area, the global interventions act mainly through projects of NGOs and associations that influence the way of living and of constructing,[1] but also through international projects of profit organizations, such as the oil and gas industry, which is bringing a skilled labour force to live on site, mainly as temporary residents. These temporary Western residents are provided with a higher standard of houses and services (such as restaurants, bars, supermarkets, shops and so on). Furthermore, the increase in the local middle class is influencing the elements of living, both at the house level, with the use of prefabricated elements, and at the neighbourhood level, with the use, for example, of cars and motorbikes. These factors are drastically changing the quality of physical and interpersonal relationships.

Today, the prevailing typology is the evolution of the traditional Swahili house for the urban settlement, but with the passage from a rural to an urban society, the lifestyle is changing, and this traditional typology is being affected. People have more dynamic lives: they move to work, inside or outside the city, they spend less time in the house and they have less time for its maintenance. Therefore, perishable vegetal materials are replaced with industrial ones that last longer. The industrial materials, such as the *chapa*[2] and objects, such as window and door frames, are considered a symbol of wealth. The quick phenomenon of urbanization and a societal predisposition to enlarged family houses lead to an increase in the number of people living within the house. The solution is the traditional house type, with an increase in the number of huts within the yard, each one with a room for one male person. In addition to this, the number of rooms within the main building is also increasing. According to Bruschi, this number will continue to increase because of the substitution of the traditional vegetal roof with the *chapa*, which is a light structure independent from the internal distribution (Bruschi, Lage, and Carrilho, 2005).

Finally, as electricity is present in most of the houses, telecommunications and the improvement in technologies are accessible to most of the population. Wi-Fi and radio antennas allow for data exchange in most of the houses as most of the people own a mobile phone and/or a smartphone, and some also have a laptop. This affects the landscape on one side, as antennas are often installed within the yard on wooden structures, and the functions performed within the house, besides increasing the knowledge and access to information of the inhabitants and the huge possibilities presented by the online world.

Notes

1 As an example, the mentioned 2016 UN Habitat and USAID project to increase inhabitants' construction skills.
2 Metal sheets, usually made from zinc, are used mainly for roofing.

Reference list

Books

Bruschi, S., Lage, L., and Carrilho, J. (2005), *Era Uma Vez Uma Palhota*. Maputo: FAPF. Faculdade de Arquitectura e Planeamento Físico-UEM, Centro de Estudos e Desenvolvimento do Habitat.

PhD thesis

Pereira, R. P. S. (2012). *Instrumento de planeamento para cidades médias moçambicanas: o caso de Pemba*. PhD University of Lisbon.

6   Conclusions

By approaching developing contexts, it is important to recognize the limit of applying the Western categories to the local reality, as they are often not recognizable or applicable, for example, the clear distinction between formal and informal or between planned and unplanned. This is because the evolutionary process of the context has given rise to specific social, urban and architectural phenomena. Having a real conscience and knowledge of these phenomena makes it possible to identify more context-specific design solutions. As mentioned in Chapter 1, according to Sarr's definition of culture (Sarr, 2018), to be sustainable, the development must be rooted in the local culture. For this reason, it is important to enhance the local cultural identity through all its forms and to provide documentation for its preservation and communication. With this study on Pemba's houses, it is possible to contribute to the enhancement of the prevailing living culture of Mozambique through the study of the selected residential neighbourhoods.

This research focussed on the need for an in-depth understanding of the connections between the house typologies and the resultant urban morphology in order to record and give to designers and planners the tools for envisioning an urban development that takes into consideration the local culture of living in its tangible and intangible aspects. Today, even the masterplan and vision for the city of Pemba do not take into account the relationship between the potentialities of the prevailing house typology and the possible urban evolution.

Believing in the validity of the UNESCO Historic Urban Landscape approach (UNESCO, 2011) and its relevance in the context of Pemba, this research links the heritage, the economic, the environmental and the socio-cultural aspects of the living context in order to allow the construction of knowledge for planning that is context specific and is able to enhance the local cultural identity.

Furthermore, in the framework of the *New Urban Agenda* (ONU, 2017), this research contributes to the development of the urban environment through the empowerment of local communities in respect to their cultural identity and their diversity,[1] for the creation of a sense of citizenship through heritage[2] and for promoting access to infrastructures and to adequate and accessible housing.

Finally, this research also addresses the Sustainable Development Goals set by the United Nations in Agenda 2030, especially for what concerns goal 2: end hunger, achieve food security and improved nutrition and promote sustainable agriculture; goal 3: ensure healthy lives and promote well-being for all at all ages; goal 6: ensure availability and sustainable management of water and sanitation for all and; goal 11: make cities and human settlements inclusive, safe, resilient and sustainable.

The main goals of this research are two-fold: firstly, to acknowledge the importance of self-built houses within the urban city fabric (as for Rapoport, 1988, p. 73) and to record the actual stage of development of the city, giving self-built architecture the dignity of being studied. Secondly, to fill the gap of knowledge on the houses' typologies and the neighbourhoods' morphology of Pemba, surveying and analyzing the characteristics of living in Pemba, trying to detect the elements that best represent the local cultural identity.

The questions that were first raised to comprehend the housing phenomenon in Pemba were: (1) What are the characteristics of living in Pemba? (2) How do the houses' typologies relate to the urban fabric and to the street, and what are the existing relationships between covered/uncovered and public/private spaces? (3) What are the features of variance and permanence from the traditional typology to the contemporary one, and how did the city development dynamics influence the houses' evolution in time?

However, these questions were defined by studying the available documentation, but after spending days and weeks in the houses and neighbourhoods, the research was enriched by unexpected information, and this widened the following analysis of the produced material and the bibliographic research. Therefore, the work could not be limited to the aforementioned questions, but it included a series of themes and reflections that are reported here.

The need for this approach is linked not only to functional and cultural aspects but also economical ones. It is crucial to take into account that Pemba cannot afford substantial public investments. Therefore, the envisioned development needs to make the most of alternative resources, such as the creativity of local inhabitants and their productive and building capabilities. For example, today the prevailing construction typology – especially due to technical reasons – does not allow for the construction of more than one floor. The resulting urban landscape is made up of the repetition of the single-storey typology with very low population density (1,400 inhabitants per km^2)[3] and a consequently high land cover. The prevalence of one-floor constructions is leading the city to a sprawl phenomenon that will increase if the expected population growth occurs. This is considered unsustainable for urban development in the historical European context, but it can represent a potential for the implementation of alternative solutions of urban development. So how can the local traditional typology be of inspiration for new city models? And how can we safeguard this knowledge? To clarify, these people, most of them illiterate and without consistent school education, have a profound knowledge of the environment in which they live, as often happens in the rural world. This competence extends also to houses; they are able to build shelters that allow them to live within the city and also to produce some food for the family's needs. In the globalized and rich world, this diffused competence does not exist anymore and is a lost richness. This is why its documentation, preservation and enhancement are needed.

Furthermore, looking closer at the dwellings and settlements issue in Pemba, it is possible to observe that, within homogeneous houses and urban fabrics typologies, a multitude of ethnic groups and cultures is present. But they share their house typology and the knowledge of how to build it. Further research questions can be raised. Is this method of building the house and the neighbourhood creating spaces that have the added value of allowing dialogue among different ethnic groups? The shift from a rural to an urban lifestyle is reinforcing the housing issue with new topics ranging from the creation of new settlements to the changes in typologies, mainly related to the use of industrial materials and an urban lifestyle. So, how can new technologies and materials be used properly to create a virtuous development system, culturally rooted, instead of just being the result of a more globalized economy and the result of the inhabitants' growing purchase power? The research, starting from the typo-morphological study of Pemba houses, tries to answer these questions in a holistic way in order to recognize and enhance a set of aspects already present in the urban organism and part of the local contemporary culture.

Another point to be highlighted concerns the methodology used for the research, the integrated analysis. This is crucial as it allows, through a plurality of elements, scales and tools of observation and an understanding of all of the factors of which the culture of living is made. As explained in depth in the dedicated chapter, this was divided into three main phases: the first one consisted of the study of the bibliographical resources and the construction of the theoretical background of the methodology. The second phase of the on-site operations dealt with the application of the survey methodology, while the third one concentrated on the integrated analysis and evaluation. The on-site survey is the crucial element of this work as it created the opportunity to document the interiors of over 50 surveyed houses with the representation of spaces, functions and objects, including interviews with inhabitants. Therefore, the selection of images presented in this research is a pure representation of the everyday life in the surveyed houses.

The surveyed typologies are significant because they are part of the local cultural heritage and represent the house's evolution from the Swahili vernacular one. They represent variations *to* a model and not *of* the model, creating a cultural landscape[4] that is uniform and stable (Rapoport, 1988, p. 70). The houses surveyed in the Alto Gingone neighbourhood are the most coherent with the Swahili typology and, in particular, one is the feature characterizing the culture of living: the position of the main building in relation to the plot boundary that creates a direct connection between the public space of the street and the private space of the house. This house type is currently changing due to several factors, such as the shift from a rural to an urban society, the possibility of buying and using industrial instead of local materials and the increase in the number of house inhabitants, primarily due to family members moving to the city for work reasons.

This house type that prevails in Alto Gingone, but that is found, even if in smaller numbers, in all of the city neighbourhoods, is part of the local traditional culture and knowledge as people have the competences for self-building it, and its general construction rules are clear. For the city management and development, self-building is an important resource as, due to the urbanization rate and the economic conditions of the country, it would not be feasible to provide housing to all of the new citizens without it. Furthermore, people recognize themselves in the lifestyle generated by this typology as it is part of their cultural identity.

Also, from a purely spatial point of view, the typology has interesting characteristics. Its internal distribution allows for easy connection between the inside and outside spaces. This connection generates a good quality of the street space, with the street fronts characterized by permeable façades instead of closed boundaries, as happens, for example, in the majority of the houses of the Natite neighbourhood.

Furthermore, in all of the neighbourhoods, the houses' elements are made mostly of local materials, which make the houses environmentally friendly and cheaper. When a family inserts an industrial element in their house façade, such as a door or a window, this is often not properly employed and sometimes is used merely as a decoration or for symbolic and religious purposes. These elements influence the typology; the main visible change today is represented by PVC roofs which, being much lighter than the vegetal ones, often modify the whole structural and distributive needs of the house.

The houses are oversized, and this is a positive aspect as it leads to a wide range of flexibility of functions within the courtyard; however, they are lacking the basic infrastructures such as water and sanitary systems.

Among the architectural and spatial elements of the typology, two main ones that increase the quality of life can be seen in the interior/exterior and public/private relationships: the courtyard and the veranda.

The courtyards of the houses are almost empty spaces, used for multiple purposes, among which is the family's food production, mainly with poultry and kitchen gardens. The courtyard, as it is conceived, creates the possibility of having a green productive space that is a resource for families and has the potential to integrate the municipal vision of agricultural implementation with a diffused productive system. Thanks to the spatial element of the courtyard, a new urban production can be envisaged, including agriculture and micro industry, which will lead to a bottom-up agricultural development instead of using top-down strategies. As a consequence of the 2019 Idai and Kenneth cyclones, this can be a strong weakness, but at the same time it increases the resilience of a community as, in many cases, inhabitants were able to rebuild their homes in a short time on their own.

The veranda is the architectural element creating a powerful interaction between the public and the private space, increasing the quality of the streets through permeable street fronts. It is present in all of the houses of Alto Gingone, and it derived directly from the Swahili typology. It stands on the two main sides of the main building, and it is used for several functions such as cooking, working and resting.

At the neighbourhood scale, it is possible to say that the typology is easily aggregable and independent from the urban structure. It can be used in this context because of people's competences, local materials and land availability. Therefore, the typology works also in its agglomeration.

Public space is present and perceived as important by the community, especially the space around the neighbourhood headquarters: today these neighbourhood centres are hosting places for public activities such as a school, trading centres, health centre, political or religious space and also spaces for social activities. Since these are the strong elements of this culture of living, within the house and the neighbourhood, how is it possible to think of the amelioration of these to be spatial drivers of the city's development? The public spaces, for example, could be reinforced in their public functions in order to become strong communitarian centres that are able to provide most of the urban services needed by the population and to minimize the need to commute to the city's central districts.

The development of the neighbourhood centres should provide, first of all, hygienic services and waste collection in order to improve the sanitary system at the neighbourhood level, reducing the phenomenon of open-air defecation and latrines in courtyards. The hygienic services should integrate the public wells network that is already present in the municipality. This implementation should be accompanied by an informative campaign on the use of the sanitary systems, basic hygienic norms to prevent illnesses and use and storage of water (drinkable and not drinkable). This could also be an occasion to inform the population about the prevention of sexual diseases, which are still among the main causes of death. The improvement of hygienic services and waste collection will also have consequences on the natural environment; it will be much cleaner, safer and more respected. These actions are aimed at raising awareness of the population about the aforementioned issues.

Envisioning the implementation of the typology as a constituent element of the urban fabric, seen in the low density of the buildings, it is fundamental to develop the infrastructural system and in particular the public transportation system, which today is almost absent and can be enriched both with traditional buses and with new sustainable systems such as bike or car sharing. This kind of development would increase the quality of life through the use and amelioration of the existing housing typology. All of these improvements function in respect to the environment and create the basis of a new concept of the city that is socially and environmentally sustainable.

Addressing these problems and finding desirable solutions will also lay the basis for a safer environment that will foster other economic activities envisioned by the municipality in its plans, in particular tourism. In fact, even though the municipality is envisaging a great touristic development, today tourism is difficult to implement outside the boundaries of the resorts' facilities, especially because of the risks related to health issues. Tourists today can enjoy the natural beauties of the city but only in a sort of ghettoization within the resorts. The resorts provide all of the infrastructures for a Western standard of comfort but do not allow a real exchange with the local culture and community. Furthermore, many potential travellers, especially those travelling for leisure and cultural purposes, do not go to Pemba because of the risk of contracting diseases, such as malaria or cholera, which can happen even if all precautions have been taken. The amelioration of the sanitary system will let more tourists come to the city and visit popular neighbourhoods that today are completely out of touristic itineraries. This change in tourism fluxes will provide the local community with a great opportunity for cultural exchange and income. The traveller, not being ghettoized anymore, will be enabled to encounter the residents, which will improve the touristic experience and therefore increase the quality of the relationship between them. A new form of tourism may evolve in Pemba, a more sustainable and ethical one, not based just on the touristic attractions but also on cultural exchange, in accordance with the United Nations World Tourism Organization (UNWTO) Global Code of Ethics for Tourism (UNWTO, 1999).

Parallelly, once the population is educated to act in respect of the basic health and environmental precautions, it will be possible to think about further interventions, such as the requalification of the seafront, for example, the one that will allow the neighbourhood of Chuiba, envisaged by the municipality, to become a touristic spot. In order to render the new area respected and long-lasting, the project of a new seafront should include at least the community sea-related activities, such as fishing and seafood collection, boat storage, commercial and leisure activities, public toilets and bathrooms.

Finally, it is important to point out the elements to be improved in the typology, going back to the UN Habitat definition of a slum:

> a group of individuals living under the same roof in an urban area who lack one or more of the following:
>
> 1 Durable housing of a permanent nature that protects against extreme climate conditions.
> 2 Sufficient living space which means not more than three people sharing the same room.
> 3 Easy access to safe water in sufficient amounts at an affordable price.
> 4 Access to adequate sanitation in the form of a private or public toilet shared by a reasonable number of people.
> 5 Security of tenure that prevents forced evictions.
>
> (UN Habitat, 2006)[5]

As already stated, most of the residential area of Pemba can be considered a slum because of the lack of three (1, 3 and 4) of the aforementioned features.

Concerning feature 1 "Durable housing of a permanent nature that protects against extreme climate conditions", the houses built with the technique of *pau à pique*[6] lack both resistance and hygiene. Since Pemba is located in a tropical zone, during the wet season the rains can be very heavy (INE, 2015, p. 15),[7] and the recent cyclonic episodes[8] demonstrate that climate extremes are hitting the area hard and that often houses do not provide a safe shelter. The inhabitants need to be informed and trained regarding the improvement of their houses, especially in relation to materials and construction technologies. Focussing on this, there are experiences of educational projects fostering their resilience that work to improve the quality and security of the constructions with a capillary working with the local communities (UN Habitat, USAID, CMCP, 2016), and this training activity should be further developed.

In relation to feature 3 "Easy access to safe water in sufficient amounts at an affordable price", most of the neighbourhoods of Pemba are provided with public water wells. In most of the cases, women and children transport, in tanks of 10 to 20 litres, the water from the well to the house, even at distances of several kilometres. The water is then left in the tanks and used for the family's daily needs. Rainwater is also collected and stored in tanks in the courtyards. However, in most cases, it is not stored in the proper hygienic conditions. Nevertheless, it is used as drinkable water, often without any kind of filtration or cleaning. Furthermore, the inappropriate storage of sweet water allows mosquitos to reproduce and therefore presents an easier diffusion of malaria.

Today the municipality is extending the pipe network, which is reaching most of the houses in the Alto Gingone and Natite neighbourhoods, and in a few years, it should reach all of the houses with a tap. However, water is scarce, especially during the dry seasons, and the creation of a desalination plant could be envisaged which would transform seawater into potable water which could be powered with photovoltaic panels. The funding of this expensive idea could be envisaged in partnership with foreign companies working in the Cabo Delgado region's LNG plantations as a compensation that could lead to a significant rise in people's living standards.

Concerning feature 4, "Access to adequate sanitation in the form of a private or public toilet shared by a reasonable number of people", the drainage system is not present in most of the neighbourhoods. Houses usually have a latrine excavated in the sand within the courtyard, located along the boundaries furthest from the house. Once the hole is filled with excrement, it is closed and a new one is opened in a different area of the courtyard. Those houses that do not follow this kind of system use the natural environment close to the house for defecation, such as the beach or fields. This custom increases the spread of other diseases, among which is cholera, which is highly affecting the city's population. Therefore, the creation of a system of neighbourhood public toilets is crucial for any kind of future perspective of the city.

In spite of these deficiencies, the houses are part of the cultural identity of the place and represent a stage of evolution of the Swahili traditional typology, and its evolution should follow its own path. As Lévi-Strauss stresses, each culture has its own path of evolution inscribed in a peculiar system of criteria that determine the process (Lévi-Strauss, 2017). Being self-built, the houses have the great power to change in a short time, and if the citizens are given the proper tools, the implementation can be quick, cheap and capillary.

These characteristics of living, both at the urban and architectural scale, can represent a strength for the development and could improve the innovation of the existing model of urbanization.

As Bruschi explains in *Era Uma Vez Uma Palhota* (Bruschi, Lage, and Carrilho, 2005), in Mozambique, mainly characterized by rural settlements, the urban culture does not really exist and has to be patiently created in respect of the habits and traditions of those who are moving from the countryside to the city, so as to guarantee the transition from a rural to an urban society without trauma.

Not having an already-established proper urban culture is perceived, in the framework of this research, not as a weakness but as strength. It is precisely in such a context, where there are no existing infrastructures of the industrial sector and where the urban culture is now being derived from the rural one, that a new concept of a city can rise and be developed.

Changing the spatial hierarchies through the implementation of the local self-built houses, and enriching them with a diffuse production, the possibility of creating a new type of city is generated in which the need for transportation, the commute time and the related economy of scale change their meaning. Therefore, density is no longer a factor that determines the concept of city, a city that integrates the urban and the rural world and that enjoys the advantages of a diffused production. This would be possible only if it is intended as a natural evolution by the citizens, and this is an additional reason why the local historical typology should be employed, so that the vernacular knowledge is not lost and people can self-build their houses and integrate them with the agricultural production instead of changing their way of living.

Notes

1 As stated in the New Urban Agenda (A/RES/71/256) "We commit ourselves to urban and rural development that is people-centred, protects the planet, and is age – and gender – responsive and to the realization of all human rights and fundamental freedoms, facilitating living together, ending all forms of discrimination and violence, and empowering all individuals and communities while enabling their full and meaningful participation. We further commit ourselves to promoting culture and respect for diversity and equality as key elements in the humanization of our cities and human settlements". p. 7/29.

2 As stated in the New Urban Agenda (A/RES/71/256) "sustainable leveraging of natural and cultural heritage [. . .] to safeguard and promote cultural infrastructures and sites [. . .] as well as traditional knowledge and the arts, highlighting the role that these play in rehabilitating and revitalizing urban areas and in strengthening social participation and the exercise of citizenship". p. 9/29.

3 Data INE 2007.

4 As Rapoport defines it, cultural landscape is the outcome of many decisions by many individuals over long periods of time, and spontaneous settlements can be considered as a particular type of it (Rapoport, 1988, p. 52).

5 UN-Habitat, State of the Worlds' Cities, 2006/7.

6 As previously explained, *pau à pique* is the prevailing construction technique employed by Pemba inhabitants for their houses. It is made of wattle and daub, two rows of bamboo sticks filled with stones and mud, earth on the ground and has a vegetal or PVC roof.

7 In 2015 in Pemba, the National Institute of Metereology recorded a minimum of 0 mm of water in September and a pick of 384,2 mm of precipitations (INE, 2015).

8 The situation created by the two cyclones Idai and Kenneth in 2019 is described in Chapter 3 of this book.

Reference list

Bruschi, S., Lage, L., and Carrilho, J. (2005). *Era Uma Vez Uma Palhota*. Maputo: FAPF. Faculdade de Arquitectura e Planeamento Físico-UEM, Centro de Estudos e Desenvolvimento do Habitat.

Lévì-Strauss, C. (2017). *L'Antropologia di fronte ai problemi del mondo moderno*. Firenze: Bompiani.

Rapoport, A. (1988). *Spontaneous Shelter*. Philadelphia: Temple University Press.

Sarr, F. (2018). *Afrotopia*. Roma: Edizioni dell'Asino.

Documents and reports

INE. (2015). *Anuario Estatistico*.

ONU. (2017). *New Urban Agenda, Quito Declaration on Sustainable Cities and Human Settlements for All*.

UNESCO. (2011). *Historic Urban Landscape Recommendation*.

UN Habitat. (2006). *State of the World's Cities 2006/7*. https://mirror.unhabitat.org/documents/media_centre/sowcr2006/SOWCR%205.pdf.

UN Habitat, USAID, Conselho Municipal da Cidade de Pemba. (2016). *Avaliação Rápida da Situação de Infra-estruturas habitacional na Cidade de Pemba no contexto de adaptação as mudanças climáticas Bairros de Paquitequete, Cariacó (Chibuabuari), Josina Machel, Chuiba e Eduardo Mondlane*.

UNWTO. (1999). *Global Code of Ethics for Tourism*.

Websites

Instituto National de Estatística | www.ine.gov.moz
UNESCO | www.unesco.org
UN Habitat | www.unhabitat.org

Index

Note: page numbers in *italic* indicate a figure and page numbers in **bold** indicate a table on the corresponding page. Page numbers followed by 'n' indicate a note.

Printed in the United States
by Baker & Taylor Publisher Services